TAROT

*Twenty-Two Steps to
a Higher Path*

D. BALOTI LAWRENCE

Photos by Phillip Collins
Cover design by Christina A. Ascione
Interior design by Donna Miller
Library of Congress Cataloging-in-Publication Data
Lawrence, D. Baloti.
    Tarot: 22 steps to a higher path/D. Baloti Lawrence.
        p. cm.
    ISBN: 0-681-41414-6
    1. Tarot.   2. Self-actualization (Psychology)—Miscellanea.
I. Title.
BF1879.T2L39   1992
133.3'2424—dc20   92-3594
ISBN: 0-681-41414-6   CIP
Printed in U.S.A.

0   9   8   7   6   5   4   3   2

Contents

Acknowledgments

My sincere thanks to the following people for their support in the conception and completion of *22 Steps to a Higher Path*.

To family and friends for their continuous understanding.
To the entire staff at Longmeadow Press for their valuable insight and judgement. To Diem Jones for his unlimited faith. Special thanks to Gloria Manley-Lawrence, M.D., for the lessons of spiritual integration. Last, but not least, for the existence of life's lessons that create joy and love on the entire planet. May we have more of them in the years to come.

This book is presented in appreciation of our higher values. It is a source of inspiration from both natural and cosmic elixers. From these forces, each of us may nourish our physical, mental, and spiritual well-being.

What is the Higher Path?

The "Higher Path" represents the progress that each of us will make during our lifetime. This progress can take the form of physical, emotional, social, financial, and especially spiritual growth. After all, these are the universal elements that each of us desire at some time or another. It seems that from the time we are born events unfold themselves daily, changing, sculpting and eventually shaping our lifestyles.

Today, many questions concerning these events are being pondered by even the least inquisitive minds. While there is a widespread interest in self-help classes such as stress management, assertiveness training and improving relationships, these are just a few of the examples of the current thirst for information and knowledge pertaining to our growth, development, and ultimate happiness.

To each individual, happiness may mean something different. For many, the maintenance of good health is essential. For others, it may be the acquisition of vast financial wealth, while some dedicate their time and energy to the pursuit of spiritual enlightenment.

Perhaps all three are important. Certainly we live in a world that places emphasis on the need for money and power. At the same time, great wealth without good health is almost meaningless. Wealth or health without some level of spiritual enlightenment, makes for a shallow existence. It appears that maintaining some level of balance between these elements provide the true meaning of "Steps to a Higher Path."

When the concept of defining this path presented itself, I thought it not only important to define what it is but also, why it is important in the life of each and every one of us.

At some point each person will find one of the aforementioned areas to have meaning. When we are sick (physically or emotionally), good health takes center stage. If bills are mounting, and financial pressures abound, the focus will be on resolving those issues. What happens however, when life seems to be a puzzle—when there seems to be no way out; when none of the puzzle pieces seem to fit? Where does our source of understanding come from?

The answers will come from an understanding of the spiritual laws. The combination of spiritual understanding and spiritual practice can be used to positively affect your physical, emotional, and social well-being.

There is no mystical, superstitious, hidden meaning to the concept of true spiritual understanding. It does not mean that you must follow a guru, wear strange clothing, or join a monastery. It does, however, mean that you must open yourself up to your deeper self—to your real self. Forget or dismantle any preconceptions, limitations and unreasonable fears. Open yourself to a place where your true and hidden potential awaits, to a place where you sensitize your hearing to hear what you could not hear before. You can only then expand your vision to see clearer, wider and farther, and increase your powers of faith, hope and self confidence to expand both your logical and intuitive powers of thinking to achieve your personal goals and the global needs of humanity as a whole.

While it is said that there are many roads which lead to the same place, you can travel only one path at a time. While traveling our individual paths we are often distracted, detoured, and even take a wrong turn from time to time. How can we stay on target, and reach our goals? How can we accomplish more and preserve our health at the same time? How can we simultaneously attract romance, and receive financial fulfillment?

This particular path which we are about to embark on is both a way of life and a method for living. The path is the process by which we obtain and maintain the things which our heart, mind, and body desire.

The higher path moves you closer to your ultimate destiny. It elevates you, provides clarity for you. As we will soon discover, there are always choices in everything we do. There is a choice that will keep us functioning from our lower selves, and there is a choice that will proliferate our higher self. As it seems, the higher we evolve on every level, the easier life becomes. We will learn to gain control over our lives, as we make decisions to stop letting people, places and things manipulate our vital energy. This is the first step to realizing the power of the self. The first step on the path is quite simply the awareness of your two beings.

Through your work with the tarot, you will hopefully connect your inner (intuitive) self with your outer (external) reality. As the journey starts a wonderful sort of union begins. It is a union of your many aspects into a cohesive whole that illuminates and amplifies everything you do.

You are not walking the path alone. The energies of those before you as well as your contemporary seekers are in full support of everything you do. In your desire to obtain truth and wisdom, you will encounter many teachers. You will yourself become a teacher for others who follow you on this path. You will become more aware than ever before of the purpose and meaning of everything in your life. Clarity will prevail over confusion, health will dominate disease, intuition will blend with logic, and hope will reign over despair.

There will be many times when you will wonder what the purpose of such a journey is, and you will even question the effect it is having in your life. At first it will seem that you are receiving no tangible results. But patience is a virtue. How well that statement rings true of the path, for it is a walkway to virtue in itself.

Many things will come and go during your journey. Part of the lesson it seems is to release falsehood and excess baggage, baggage that is not your own. Accepting and confronting truth over falsehood will bring you from the dark of escapism and deceit to the bright light of confrontation and resolution, releasing you from obstacles and bad habits that hinder your progress.

The "Higher Path" is a roadmap to our physical, emotional, spiritual, social, and material well-being. It is the road we must walk to maintain a sense of self integrity, and resourcefulness. It is the way in which we will rise above the mundane but at the same time master the practical issues in our daily life. Most important, the road we walk as individual beings is the same one which connects us to the universal elements and the God–like consciousness of our mission.

This is an invitation for you to explore your higher path. A challenge for you to open your mind and your senses to experience life to the fullest. An opportunity to enhance your physical, mental, spiritual, social, and economic well-being. Welcome to The Higher Path!

What is the Tarot?

The tarot is a method used to access information relating to your past, present, and future. It is a system for creating a connection between your conscious and subconscious minds, by analyzing the people, places, and things that affect your life. The tarot makes visible facts that can affect our progress to the higher path. As a method for making predictions it has become a popular tool.

Through the tarot we can learn to identify different obstacles that we might encounter and direct ways to overcome them. There are many lessons to be learned on our journey towards self-awareness. Some we learn the hard way, some the easy way. Each time we learn and apply a new lesson, we take another step forward on the path to higher consciousness, another step closer to understanding and completing our true purpose and real identity. But what is the purpose of knowing the true identity, why complete our true purpose?

Perhaps as we set about to answer these important questions, en route we will help you to understand the inner workings of the tarot system.

After you have gained an understanding of yourself—your true self—you begin to see reality from a clear perspective. Often, many of us live in the shadows of peer pressures and expectations that are reflective of our personal desires. How many times have we been influenced or persuaded to commit actions against our better judgment, only to later regret not listening to that little voice, which said no in the first place. That inner voice had the correct solution all along. Remaining centered in who we are provides each person with an inner confidence, enabling the inner voice to be not only heard, but listened to. Inner confidence is the catalyst to making choices and decisions in your life that are for the best, decisions free of fear, greed, jealousy, and other emotions that may eventually create negative circumstances. These negative circumstances may not be realized immediately, but somewhere, at some time, they will return to affect your life. Call this karma if you like, or even "reaping what you sow." The point is that every time we choose the lower path over the higher path, a dear price will be paid. The world is one large space. Everything in it is interconnected. Every time a tree is destroyed it affects the total balance of the earth. Every time a decision is made it affects the entire group. It is clear that decisions made with loving, positive intent, are more powerful and constructive than decisions made from the negative sides of our personality. Through the tarot we can gain valuable insight about our true personality, our true likes and dislikes, and our deepest feelings about certain issues. We can learn to face and confront certain realities which may otherwise be difficult for us.

The lower self is riddled with deceit and false intentions that will result in false happiness. It is a state that keeps us pretending that things are fine, when actually they are far from it. Being true to oneself, being aware of one's true self is the right direction to genuine health and wealth. As we approach the twenty-first century, the glow of enlightenment lives with us more than ever before. The conditions are ripe for a greater understanding of the personal self and of humankind as a whole. The focus all over the planet is shifting to include a new system of values which may have been unheard of in the past. We are beginning to appreciate the values of the heart, and finding that they can work alongside values of the bank account.

Love, compassion, understanding, and patience can be as rewarding as values of selfishness, envy, and violence. Quiet though it is kept, they are far more rewarding! Learning when to negotiate instead of demanding can sometimes have its advantages. Knowing how to love instead of how to hate is a reflection of the higher self. Breaking free of self-imposed limitations is like having an understanding of the true self, helping us to develop the value of patience. That will reward us in everything we do.

So many times we look for excuses for our failures or unhappiness. Through the tarot we can learn to focus just a bit more on our own inadequacies, to locate the places where we can do better. Just imagine how wonderful it would be to stop playing games with yourself and progress in every single area of your life.

The tarot can help tie together threads of isolated information to help show the entire picture. The joy of simply putting the puzzle together is exciting. Gathering each piece. Looking it over. Finding out where it fits. Watching it complete itself piece by piece, step by step.

There are several terms which seem to echo the central theme of the tarot system. Since it is a practical approach to learning by doing, the more you experience it the clearer each meaning becomes to you. Clarity and focus are repeated throughout the tarot meanings. It is through clarity that we are able to discern truth from fiction. It is through focus that we are able to zero in on our real goals, and remain on track until they are reached. By asking the cards a question or a series of questions the process of self interaction is initiated. Often one question will lead to the asking of several questions. Keep in mind the more you interact with the tarot cards, the more they begin to interact with you. In fact, there are often times when it may seem that the tarot is guiding you not only to the answers, but telling you what questions to ask. The best way to describe this process is "interactive."

The cards respond to your approach and then take it one step further. Often the cards will ask you to rephrase your question, or present it with more clarity and focus. The irony of the whole matter is that this in itself is an answer to your initial question. Your process of insight begins as you are requested to rethink exactly what you want to know. As you do this, you already gain information by seeing your situation clearer in your own mind. There are times when having more focus will allow us to answer many of our own questions. By the same token, there are times when a lack of clarity will create havoc and confusion in our minds.

Another key to understanding the concept of the tarot is that of divination—the process of foretelling the future by employing some or all phases of the intuitive senses. Tarot reading itself is a method of divination. It is a passageway into the unknown. It helps illuminate and highlight information from the subconscious aspects of knowledge.

It remains important to remind you that intuition is not the only faculty involved in any of these areas. While it is true that we need to develop our intuitive faculties and that we must have more trust in their utilization, logic still has its place. The idea of gaining complete knowledge involves a healthy balance between intuition and logic, between the conscious mind and the subconscious mind. This balance will lead to a discovery of the truth in a more efficient manner. Some have chosen to place limitations on their abilities by simply adhering to the logical process in total. Others have chosen to similarly limit their abilities by placing total faith in the intuitive process. Perhaps it is not reasonable to eliminate any function of higher learning. One of the most precious gifts of the human being is the ability to shift between the rational and the creative.

There is a most interesting connection between the tarot and reality. On the one hand it is a direct reflection of reality. On the other hand, it extends beyond reality. Keeping in mind intuition and logic must work hand in hand, enough information can be gathered concerning people, places and things in your life, to predict certain outcomes. This may sound like common sense, but in most cases we under–utilize our abilities to arrive at such conclusions.

The main purpose of this section is to start your thought process, to stimulate you to remain open to new possibilities and exciting ways of applying your highest potential. It is to explore the unexplored, creating for you a tool that can be applied in every area of your life.

Once you begin to approach the tarot you will find much of the information you receive is common sense. The fact remains, however, that obstacles, insecurities and simple stress create blinders that block out the answers to our questions.

This journey through the tarot is a journey through the realities of life. As we progress to a happier life we must learn many lessons. These lessons are reflected in the meanings of the tarot cards. Thus, by following the information hidden in their symbols, reaching our goals may become easier. The steps in the tarot are in fact a journey to a higher path.

As you travel inward, you will undoubtedly rediscover facts concerning your personality that you had forgotten or never realized before. As you journey outward, you will become more aware of your home environment—family, friends, co-workers and all other external elements. You will begin to see all these things in a different light, hopefully with more wisdom and understanding to apply to each. After all, one of the best rewards from the tarot experience is that it offers the discovery of love and wisdom, both at their highest levels and in their true form. Both can be applied by you, in social and personal relationships, with the intention of making them more fruitful and beneficial for all. Remember, the best results are gained when your intentions include love, wisdom, and the desire to help, offer service, and spread love whenever possible. Love, as it seems, is the most powerful force on earth. It is the ultimate healer. Since it is easy to misuse the information received through the tarot, my best advice is to make sure your intentions are always positive. Never try to manipulate, do harm, or seek revenge with your new found source of knowledge. Understanding why and how things work, will provide you with an upper hand in many situations. Of course, everything you do can benefit you. Just make sure that in the process, you do not harm anyone else. Since many people live in a constant state of anxiety, it's not difficult to manipulate this information to obtain a desired result. In the long run however, through the logical law of cause and effect, the last laugh will be on you should you be unwise in your use of the tarot. Use it wisely. The tarot can be great fun. It should not replace your personal growth or ability to process advanced information. Instead it should assist it. Promote it. Elevate it. Quicken it.

3

History of the Tarot

THE ORIGIN OF THE TAROT dates back thousands of years. The books of the ancient Egyptians told the story of the deity Thoth. From the book of Thoth we can see many similarities to the present symbolism found in modern tarot decks. This has led many historians to make a connection between Egyptian occult thought and the tarot.

The Tarot is composed of symbols, images, numbers, and even colors. There is often a repetition of these images found throughout the study of many cultures. It is then fair to assume that the actual process of divination is inclusive rather than exclusive of nearly all cultures. In the same way that the story of the immaculate conception repeats itself in many religions, the story behind the tarot has a similar connection across time and cultures.

How convenient the tarot is for creating such connections. It is through the card's symbols and meanings that we are able to realize the unity of this world and all its inhabitants. While the American Indians used the powers of animal images, or the Egyptians created symbolic numbers, and the Italians used royal noblemen and women, the common thread is the story behind the images. There are too many types of tarot decks in existence to describe them all. For the sake of being brief

and preserving clarity, the focus of this book will remain on what is
called the Ryder-Waite deck. As long as we understand the universal
oneness of mind, an understanding of the tarot and its development
will be complete, regardless of the idiosyncratic differences an individual deck might have.

Of special note is the relationship of the Tarot philosophy to the
study of the Kabbalah. As a system of self discovery and unity of mind,
the Kabbalah has its origins in the teachings of the Torah, the classic
book of Judaism. Early occultists have planted seeds that show some
correlation between the two philosophies. No doubt once again the use
of allegories and symbols has helped to shape such connections. Just as
the Kabbalah contains information on reaching the higher path, so do
the symbols of the tarot show the way. Just as the Egyptian Book of
Thoth refers to the symbolism of numbers and their deepest meanings,
the Kabbalah refers to the use of the Hebrew alphabet. In the Kabbalah,
as in most ancient symbolism, the use of meditation and focus is key. It
is key to opening the doorway to the path. Concentration will lead to
focus just as reflection and sensory awareness will lead to meditation.
Translations of the tarot include correlations between the Hebrew let-
ters and their meanings. In this book we will expand all those meanings
to present a more practical and current understanding.

It is my opinion after several decades of research, that all ancient
philosophies and practices have a connection in more ways than one.
There is a space where the deeper meaning of numbers, colors, symbols, shapes, patterns, and sounds cross reference one another. That is,
they all tell a single story of purpose, direction and temperament. As
the Kabbalah connects the individual mind with the God—like consciousness, the major similarity is evident—the presence of the one,
the unity of all matter, and the higher principles of human dynamics,
all reflecting the destiny of our search for higher learning.

You see that some of the cards portray what appear to be male
images, while others portray female images. Some portray older people
while others show images of younger people. There is a double meaning to the portrayal of such images. If a card shows a certain image, this
may or may not mean it is of that gender. Remember, the cards often
represent hidden meanings and are symbolic in their visual images.
Often a male card can represent the masculine side of a female, just as a
female card can relate to the feminine side of a male. Masculine and
feminine do not have to mean man and woman. There is a more complete meaning to these terms.

The universe is full of opposites. This is a scientific law. For every front there must be a back. When there is up there is down. Cold is opposite from hot. Good is opposite from bad, just as life is opposite from death. There are parts of both opposites in all things. The idea of progress and happiness is to maintain a balance. You will see that even death is not necessarily bad. In order to grow new healthy cells, the old ones must die. Before we can totally integrate positive habits into our lives, the old bad ones must leave.

Male and female energies exist in all of us. These energies are the things that keep us in balance. The oriental philosophers call this balance yin and yang. While intuition is primarily a feminine characteristic, the application of intuition is a masculine trait. Do not allow yourself to be narrow minded about these facts. We are not talking about man vs. woman, or child vs. adult. We are simply pointing out the elements necessary for all of us to maintain a healthy balance. Thus, as you understand more about the cards, you will learn in your readings that each person contains both masculine or logical energies, and each person contains feminine or intuitive powers. The irony of this is that many men utilize more feminine or yin energies, just as many women operate from a masculine or yang perspective. It is true that selecting a card with a man or a woman can represent just that, but at the same time it can represent the need for that person to acquire more of the energies suggested by that card.

Many of the cards speak of the duality of life. This duality is also reflected in the literature of every culture. Some know it as the male and female energies. It has been called yin and yang. Others know it as good and bad, or as heaven and hell.

The Kabbalah involves something called The Tree of Life. There are ten steps in the tree and like the tarot the idea is a progression from step one to the end of the path. Each step has a name, a number, and a symbolic number that represents its meaning. In between each step there are pathways that lead to the steps. These pathways, once again like in the tarot, represent the way to reach the steps. Contained in the pathways are also hidden meanings and messages on achieving progress in our lives. The similarities in the Kabbalah and the tarot are no coincidence. Early occultists who refined the tarot system, noted that the twenty-two passageways in the Kabbalah relate to the twenty-two major arcana in the tarot. The four sections of the Kabbalah which represent the four worlds relate to the four suits, wands, discs, swords, and cups of the tarot, and of course, the purpose of both is to present a method for the seekers to achieve balance and harmony in all aspects of their internal and external worlds.

Now let us take a brief tour through the development of the tarot system. I say brief because to extend it any further would mean an examination of every early culture known to us. A few are however worth noting.

As we have seen, each civilization has its own system of card reading and divination. There are some ancient Indian playing cards that have a striking resemblance to the tarot. The images in one deck are also displayed in four suits, containing pictures of Indian deities, and even have court cards reflecting symbols similar to the minor arcana. Like the Kabbalah and the tarot they contain the symbolism of numbers to help explain the full context of their meanings. Similar cards exist in China, Korea, and Egypt. Many historians believe that much of the ancient wisdom contained in these systems was initially carried from Egypt to the rest of the world, where the concepts were reshaped to fit each country's understanding and culture.

A distant relative of the tarot is certainly the game deck we know as playing cards. Their fifty-two cards including king, queen, and jack are compatible to the tarot's minor arcana, both in number and in suit. Even the extra card of the regular playing cards, descriptively called the joker, is remarkably similar to the tarot card known as the Fool.

The existence of regular playing cards seems somehow related to the development of the tarot deck. Many people who read cards today also read with the regular playing deck. Here are some associations between the two decks.

Tarot	Regular
king	king
queen	queen
knight	knight
wands	clubs
coins	diamonds
swords	spades
cups	hearts
fool	joker
ace-ten	ace-ten
56 in minor arcana	52 in total deck

Once you become adept at interpreting your subconscious thoughts, take a look at the regular playing cards and listen as they too speak to you.

It is thought that the oldest deck of actual tarot cards still in existence is the Visconti-Sforza deck, designed for the Visconti and Visconti-Sforza families. In 1392 the King of France received a pack of tarot cards painted by Jacquemin Gringonneur for his amusement. All were hand painted and displayed the artistic style of the period. Interestingly, the meanings of the cards at the superficial level have certainly been the theme of artists, musicians, and writers throughout history. During the fourteenth century, actual hand painted tarot cards surfaced in both Italy and France. The decks contained a various number of cards, until their refinement in later time periods. It is interesting to note that most of the older tarot decks used Roman numerals.

There are several theories explaining the origin of the word "tarot." The most likely has it as a root of the early word tarocchi meaning trumps or triumphs. European card makers called themselves tarotiers, a similar form of the word tarot.

It is doubtful the initial intent for the tarot was divination or prediction, although by the nineteenth-century they were in widespread use for this purpose. Elias Levi was a scholar and spiritual philosopher. As an Abbe of the Roman Catholic Church he was interested in the studies of the ancient Egyptians, Greeks, and Hebrews. He wrote of the vast spiritual connections in the tarot, and its connections to past systems of self discovery. It was he who made the important connection between the tarot and the Kabbalah. His first and most famous work "Dogme et Rituel de la Haute Magic" (Dogma of Ritual and High Magic), outlined the inspiration and true purpose of the tarot. It should be noted that Elias Levi was born Alphonse Louis Constant, but changed his name to reflect his spiritual philosophy. It was, just as it is today, a very common occurrence to select an enlightened name after such studies.

Others, such as Gerard Encausse (1865-1917) who wrote under the spiritual name of Papus, made a strong connection between the tarot and the philosophy of India. He was a French physician who assimilated both science and cosmic influences into his philosophy.

About the same time, such secret orders as the Masonic Order and the Rose-Cross were growing among the scientific and spiritual communities. The integration of both science and spirituality has been a natural marriage since the earliest civilizations. Naturally, there are always the dogmatic skeptics who frown upon such unions, however, truly intelligent and spiritual persons have always found ways to override them.

Another secret study group, known as the Hermetic Order of the Golden Dawn, was founded in England around 1887. It was a way-station for some of the more advanced western philosophers of the day. The group, which included Aleister Crowley, studied a variety of subjects including the Kabbalah, physics, astrology, celestial travel, alchemy, and self discovery. Another member of the group, Arthur Edward Waite, published "The Pictorial Key to The Tarot." The book included a deck of cards with pictures drawn by another member, Pamela Colman Smith. At the time living in England, she was a well-known American artist, while Waite was a philosopher and occultist. Published in 1910, by Rider & Company, this deck became known as the Rider-Waite Deck. Perhaps the main influence on modern tarot practices, Waite integrated the Kabbalah, and refined the meanings of the cards. Together, they developed a seventy-eight card pack that is in wide use today. It was his philosophy that the tarot was a symbol of universal ideas, inclusive of all human thought and potential.

Today, the cards are reissued by U.S. Games Systems in Connecticut. They contain authentic detail and color.

Although tarot cards are now found in German, French, Swiss, Italian, and Spanish, the majority of the decks are printed in English. "Fortune tellers" traveled throughout Europe during the 19th and 20th centuries calling themselves Gypsies. They often traveled in caravans, reading tarot cards and using other forms of divination as they moved from place to place. Some were thought to possess special powers to see into the future. Others were described as charlatans who used gimmicks and tricks. There is a very thin line between legitimate future forecasting and pure hocus pocus. One should indeed be careful about confusing the two. So-called mystics and magicians often resort to sleight of hand, and mental manipulation to persuade believing customers. Keep in mind, the need for the human spirit to move beyond the mundane is stronger than ever. People are seeking answers. Answers to solve their romantic problems. Answers to clarify career problems. Answers to resolve interpersonal insecurities and fears.

It is therefore conceivable that tarot reading will become even more popular. Much of the fog has lifted from ritualistic ceremonies of the past. The tarot has become a widely accepted tool.

Tarot Use for Everyday Living

The tarot can be utilized in your everyday life to help you move closer to your real wants and needs. It is not a panacea or miracle worker. It is not the total answer in itself. It is not a higher power that responds to the wave of a magic wand. It is not even magic.

Today, there is a vast and growing interest in the tarot. The cards are used by people in all walks of life. Tarot decks are available in many book stores, health food stores and metaphysical-book stores.

The deck contains seventy-eight cards. This includes twenty-two Major Arcana and fifty-six Minor Arcana. Each card reflects some area of our life. Not only does the tarot encourage you to search for the deeper meaning of issues, it allows you a system for focus and resolution of those issues.

The merits of divination techniques do not include being replacements for our basic common sense. The idea is not to take the place of real thinking, or to create a substitute for individual creativity. There are some who decide to ask the tarot everything. As with all things, balance is the true key to proper use of the tarot. There are times when the tarot will be a welcome associate. Just as there are times when it is best left alone.

As you analyze and reassess your life, you may find certain tools helpful in creating new aspects. Perhaps your life needs a new look, perhaps it does not. In the event it does, you will appreciate the opportunity to change it as you see fit. We sometimes live with the notion that things cannot be changed, that we are powerless to change the circumstances we are not pleased with.

Before you begin learning about the cards and their actual meanings, it won't hurt to create the conditions that will yield the best results. A major concern is your belief that you can control your life. This means you do have the power to say no, or to say yes at your own discretion. It means you are a living, breathing entity on this planet, with the right to determine your own destiny.

Faith is another concern. In order to tap into the power of higher forces, you must have faith. Faith is the belief that there is a higher power. There are forces at work, which we cannot readily see, hear, or touch, but they are there. All you need to do is have the faith to allow them to work for you.

There is a difference between faith and blind faith. Blind faith is an act which lacks common sense and direction. It often includes superstitious beliefs in some nonexistent magical powers. There is nothing magical or superstitious about the powers of faith. Believe in yourself. Believe in your abilities to have the things you desire. Use your faith wisely, it will serve you well.

A third concern is intent. You must always approach the tarot with the proper intent. Now that we have regained access to advanced techniques and information, we have a responsibility to never misuse these powers. There are people who act like children with a new toy, misusing and manipulating information. You can get what you want, but only if it does not interfere with the rights of another. You can expand your personal freedoms, but only if this expansion does not detract from the freedom of someone else. By all means you should never use the tarot when angry, anxious, or to pursue any form of revenge or harm to another. This is not the way to use the power of light granted to you through your faith.

I find it important to include this information, as it is a preamble to your journey on the higher path. These are only a few of the rules that you should adhere to. You will find that like the ten commandments, the tarot is a lesson of selflessness, not one of selfishness. It is through the act of sharing that all your dreams will come true.

It is however a set of valuable lessons that will increase your understanding. It is a journey from darkness into the light. It is a personal tool available for you to connect the inner reality of your wants and desires with the outer reality of their manifestation.

Welcome to the world of The Higher Path through the Tarot!

How Does the Tarot Actually Work?

Now that we have moved beyond any misconceptions regarding the tarot, we can begin to penetrate into the inner workings and the essence.

The tarot is a reflection of your inner mind. It is also a mirror image of the events taking place around you. When you do a reading, you are asking that those events present themselves for your clarity and understanding. The tarot is like reading a great novel that becomes more interesting as it unfolds.

Each card has several meanings. There is the general meaning, which you will find is similar in most tarot books. Then there is the special meaning, which relates to the specific questions you ask. Lastly, you will find the meaning you intuitively discover during your examination of the cards. The first two meanings become standard after a while and you will soon know them by memory. The last meaning will be more reflective of the time, place and current situation surrounding your reading.

You will find when asking the tarot for answers, that how you ask your question has a great deal to do with what your answer will be. Often you will be asked by the cards to rephrase or restate your original question. As you participate in your session your mind will expand as it becomes more receptive. Receptivity will justly lead to an openness of spirit and of heart, placing you in the proper frame of mind to accept its messages.

The tarot acts as a graphic road map of awareness. It provides prime directives into our life-cycles. In addition it displays possibilities to us, and connections linking our wants, needs and desires. Perhaps most important of all, the tarot lays the foundation for our spiritual growth. It is yet another way to receive advanced information on the path ahead, pointing out possible obstacles, and ways of progressively resolving such obstacles.

Meditation, dreams, and psychic impressions may provide a glimpse into the unseen realities of life. In the case of dreams, our mind is fed information concerning the past, present, and future which can usually be an indication of a direction for us to follow. Dreams for some of us, are a way of channeling realities into concrete form. As they appear in the subconscious mind, the images and feelings are shaped into concepts of reality.

Concentration and a reflective attitude are required for the reception of subconscious thoughts. I would like to point out here the method for receiving these thoughts requires certain mental and physical conditions. Clarity and relaxation are two of the conditions. If we are anxious, upset, angry, or exhausted, thought forms are weakened or even blocked. To have a clear reception the mind and body should be as free of tension as possible. An uptight body will block reception just as a closed mind will. Through the process of relaxation, the body and mind looses its fear, prejudice, and subjective perspective. How in the world can we receive the truth if we are blind to it, closed to it, and in fear of it?

Each of us has individual lessons to learn. Some of the lessons are continuations from previous lifetimes. Other lessons are created during this lifetime. Lessons should not be viewed as tasks or arduous procedures. They are instead, keys to freedom; techniques and methods to remove limitations. Lessons facilitate growth and the development of our higher selves. While many of us spend time complaining and feeling sorry for ourselves, others have learned to confront their shortcomings, accept them, and move on to the next step. Crying over spilled milk, always acting defensive, or always blaming ourselves or others accomplishes little. The purpose of mistakes is to learn from them. Learn and not repeat them.

As the tarot speaks, you will find it speaks especially to you, addressing your particular needs and desires. It tailors its approach to meet your individual personality. This is not exceptional, for when you begin to accept the inner quest you will discover the answers to many of your questions. You will begin to recognize the answers to many of your problems, and the solutions to many of your puzzles. Working with the tarot is like having a conversation between you and you, between your inner and outer personalities.

With each look at a tarot card, you will see several images. After a while these images will become pictures. As you continue to view them, the pictures will become stories. Finally the stories will become concepts from which your job is to extract the meanings.

As you walk through your tarot reading you will experience it as a moment of clarity and focus. A time out from the hectic fast pace. A moment of introspection and self-focus. A moment of meditation geared to reflect the hidden messages in your life.

The action of the tarot cards remains dormant until you breathe life into it. It is the assertion of your inquiries that give it full life and meaning. Until that time the tarot is simply a deck of cards with colorful pictures. It is the unity of your emotional, physical and spiritual energy that give the tarot cards motion. They begin to interact with you in a give-and-take relationship.

This give-and-take becomes personal the moment you ask for a reply. If you are doing a reading for someone else, it should be their energy the cards reply to. In Chapter 11, "how to do a reading," we will discuss these techniques further. Once again we should keep in mind the universal application of the tarot.

It can correspond to the changes in life as experienced by all human beings. There are images from the tarot which reflect our individual changes and images which reflect the changes of the planet as a whole. We call the latter universal principles.

As you now prepare yourself for experiencing the tarot, try to keep one thing in mind. It is the key to unlocking your higher powers, through reflection, receptivity, relaxation, and an objective state of mind.

The tarot is a link to the expression of your higher self. It is the roadway for you to walk the higher path. Never be afraid to follow your intuition. Never fear the true expression of your heart. It is through the discovery of the self that you will remove the obstacles confronting your success and happiness.

As you begin your readings do not try to get it all at once. You will find the information you are in search of will come. Some of it comes immediately. Some of it comes down the road.

As you learn to place your learned personality in the background, the result will bring your true self to the foreground. The same happens with those you read for. The search, remember, is for the true self. This is the self that links us to the outer world and to other people. It is the self which finds the courage and openness to express universal love. You will experience special moments during your readings. These moments have been described as "being in the world but not of it." Time, space, and place are transcended, as you begin to create your own reality. This place is the center of truth and reality.

The motivation for survival in the material world, the everyday life, will often lead you to ask questions regarding love, romance, career, or finances. This is normal, in the beginning. As you progress, your understanding will include the elements necessary to maintain these "things," The focus will be on what you should do to improve your perspective, a perspective that includes emotional, physical, and spiritual, well-being. Such a focus is not the same thing as selfishness. Selfishness is a limiting, self-centered perspective. To focus on yourself in this context does mean to find the ways and means to improve yourself from the inside out. This is the reason for placing the selfish ego and the immature parts of your personality in the background, out of the way of progress, away from the visual field, where it only serves to limit and block your true capacity. Through the Lovers card we are taught the value of relationships and the art of manifesting genuine love in these relationship. Just as love remains the most creative force available to us, the misuse of this force extends from the assertiveness of the ego or personality. Once again a valuable lesson gained from the tarot is that of balance. The balance of male and female energies. The balance of power and patience, or the balance of knowing when something is too much versus when it is too little. Balance and harmony in all things will clear the path to progress.

For those who have been enlightened, on one or all levels, the tarot offers the way to maintain that enlightenment, and to take it further. For those who stand tentatively on the border of enlightenment, you will experience the courage and belief necessary to move forward with your journey. Finally for those who have yet to give consideration to the higher path, you will be introduced to the philosophy of true knowledge for the first time.

Whoever you are, and at whatever place you are on the path, Welcome. May it be a pleasant and rewarding journey for you!

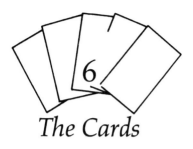

6

The Cards

MAJOR ARCANA

The Major Arcana are the strongest cards in the deck. Their meanings have earned them respect and sheer power when one is drawn. There are twenty-two Major Arcana. In the Rider-Waite deck, the cards begin with the Fool (number zero) and end with the World (number twenty-one). The Major Arcana represent the most important aspects of an issue. When a Major Arcana shows up in a reading, it requires special attention because it is often the main lesson we are to learn at that particular sitting. It is a close reflection of the natural laws of the universe. More to the point are each of the Major Arcana and their close representation of our actual personalities. At some time in our life, we will experience each of the principles of the Major Arcana. No matter who we are, where we live, our sex, religion, or belief system, the Major Arcana shows us the way. The experiences tell the story of our deepest secrets and hold the hidden treasures of knowledge.

If you have already purchased your deck of cards, here is your first exercise. Separate the Major from the Minor Arcana. Lay the Major Arcana out on a table in front of you. Put them in order beginning with the Fool and ending with the World. As you relax and meditate on the cards take note of the following:

1. The colors in each card help tell a story. While red may represent action and activity, blue may suggest the need for peace and inner reflection.

2. Remember the number of each card. As we will discuss in a later chapter, each number represents a series of experiences. For example,

four is the need to complete projects, while eight symbolizes material profit and wealth.

3. Who are the other images portrayed in each card? What is their significance? The Lovers are portrayed with an angelic figure hovering above, perhaps representing inspiration or the need for truth in maintaining a successful relationship.

4. Which direction are the figures headed? Are they leaving the area or coming into the area? Are they headed away from the main event or are they coming into the main event? Are they pointing upward or is their attention downward?

5. Many of the cards show natural elements, such as mountains, clouds, or bodies of water. Others have animals, while still others show the use of various types of clothing.

6. What is the astrological or planetary influence of the card? While the influence of the Hermit is the sign of Virgo, Aries is the Emperor's ruler.

Each and every symbol has a meaning. At the start, you will not be expected to know all the meanings of every symbol. Just focus on the ones that strike your attention first. They will be the ones that have the most meaning to you. At each reading, a different image may assert itself. During some readings the cards will appear to speak to you loud and clear. During other readings, they will seem foggy and evasive. Not to worry! Keep relaxing and meditating on your cards and eventually you will see what you need to.

It is through the Major Arcana that you can alter your destiny. As each card speaks to you of the qualities associated with it, your higher ideals may become a conscious projection through meditation on it. It is through the Major Arcana that we possess the possibility for change and growth.

Another definition for the Major Arcana is "major facts," while the Minor Arcana relates to "minor facts."

As you look at the Major Arcana you might want to begin drawing your own conclusions about them. See what each means to you. Ask yourself as many questions as you can. Allow your mind to move into the card. Be creative, flow with the meaning of the card.

Through the Major Arcana your reading will be given a strong influence and focus. It is focus which makes the tarot so effective. It is the path from darkness into light. It is the illumination of higher aspirations and ideals. Each of our higher ideals are projected in one of the Major Arcana. It is the Major Arcana that connects our mental, spiritual and physical selves.

As a clue to their meanings each card has a special title. Even the card name implies the power and meaning of the card, names such as the Sun, which brings warmth and sunshine to a situation, or the Hermit which implies the need for solitude and inner reflection in the search for wisdom. Each card is exciting and highly visual, with graphic, colorful images.

By all means, do not let yourself be confused or entangled in the historical references to the mysticism and ancient beliefs of their time period. Keep in mind the cards were developed in the early part of this century. While some of the images seem dated, they still reflect the universality of truth as we know it.

In the Major Arcana you will find the answer to many of your questions. Use the cards wisely. Accept the truth when it is favorable to you, and be wise enough to accept the truth when it is not as favorable to you. In the Major Arcana you will discover the secret to unlocking doors you once thought impossible to open.

MINOR ARCANA

The Minor Arcana should not be taken lightly. Although it is true the Major Arcana tells the major story, the Minor Arcana help refine and clarify the story. It crosses the t's, dots the i's, and puts the punctuation marks in all the right places.

The Minor Arcana is divided into four suits. You will find several names for these suits. We choose to use Pentacles, Wands, Swords, and Cups.

There are actually fifty-six cards in the Minor Arcana. Forty are regular cards of the suit and sixteen are royal or court cards. The regular cards are numbered in each suit, ace to ten, while the royal cards include the page, knight, queen, and king of each suit.

Like the Major Arcana, each card is a colorful and visual representation of several meanings. Each suit represents a force in nature, and the characteristics of that force.

Wands represent the element of fire. They are exciting, active, and stimulating. They also relate to business endeavors and new projects. Aggressiveness, business acumen, courage, and honor are their character traits. In the regular playing card deck, they imply clubs. Growth and movement is also indicated. Happiness, joy, and laughter surround the wands. Leadership, boldness, and spontaneous behavior are more traits of the wands. New, birth, start, engine, power, strength, masculine, heat, summer, red, first chakra, Mars, Jupiter, Aries, Leo, Sagittarius, musical tone of c, natural and circulation are words which correspond with the aspect of the wands. Wands also connect with war, violence, innocence, passion, the sun, straightforward, and ego.

Swords represent the element of air. They symbolize new ideas, logical thinking, action, movement, travel, and our efforts to manifest. Wands give movement to our ideas manifested by the thoughts of the swords. They also indicate the obstacles and struggles we face in reaching our goals. From the swords we exercise our intellect, mental energy, and logical thinking. It is the force of communication, writing, speaking, inventiveness, and discrimination. Swords will allow for the releasing of old or negative energies in our life. It is the method of shaping and refining our wants and desires. Misusing the power of the sword will often lead to danger, violence or disaster. The mind is, after all, a powerful tool in itself. Swords represent Aquarius, Libra, and Gemini. They can cleanse, or reach into, places other tools cannot. Ideas, decisions, logic, inventions, journeys, space travel, lightness, quickness, memory, learning, study, higher education, accounting, light blue and green, white, and expansion are words that connect with the aspect of the swords. In the regular playing-card deck they connect with spades. Swords are also linked with nobility and the military. Their attitudes can be aloof, detached, and superficial. Swords also connect with oxygen, wind, and cold. It is through the use of the sword that we expand into super realms of consciousness, and create the higher ideals of humanity.

Pentacles   represent earth. They reflect stability, organization, and firmness. Virgo, Capricorn, and Taurus understand the inner working of the pentacles. Money, practicality, reality, and learned knowledge reflect the pentacles. Commerce, business, negotiation, barter foundation, status quo, taskmaster, determination, simplicity, patience, industry, government, managerial, import-export, depth, hands on, and career are words that respond to the symbolism of the pentacles. They are often referred to as coins. Pentacles represent the ability to finish what we start and hold fast under all adversity. As with all suits, the pentacles are not without their cautions. As they are slow to accept change, pentacles reflect the lesson of moving on with the times. They can also represent mountains, valleys, meadows, deserts, and agriculture. Their purpose includes the sharing of physical energy for health, and well-being for the physical body. They live in the real world. A world of mundane and step by step procedures. They like to see, touch, feel, and hold what they encounter. Pentacles also help us with removing greed, the feeling of being stuck, and being too critical. Pentacles help make ideas a reality. After the seed of an idea is created by the swords, and given sunlight by the wands, it begins to grow from the earth, awaiting the nourishing waters of the cups. Pentacles are the foundation of an issue. The bottom line, the actuality of an issue is the understanding reflected by the pentacles. If you select a card of this suit it may mean you should pay more attention to detail and the actual facts of an issue.

Cups   represent the element of water. They reflect the need for love, emotions, and intuition in our lives. Cups connect with the water signs of Pisces, Cancer, and Scorpio. They can be a river, a stream, or the deep ocean. Cups seem to portray the creative arts, dance, poetry, music, and theater. Intuitive, mystery, fluid, penetrating, mutable, chemicals, perfumes, service, hospitals, therapies, counselors, inspiration, nourishment, emotions, spiritual, creation, pleasure, romance, happiness, celebrations, illusions, kindness, religions, and beauty are words that associate with the cups. Whenever the cups come up in a reading it signifies the need to balance or apply an intuitive approach to a situation. Perhaps one where the heart balances the intellect. Or as in the reverse the need to keep the emotions in check when they have gone out of control. As the earth (pentacles) creates a foundation for the growing of the seed, the cups (water) will nourish it as it pours its fertile nutrients upon it. Of course this applies to romance, relationships, business, or creative ideas. Cups are the emotional aspect of our lives. Cups remind us of the ability to flow through changes in our life without attempting to always escape or hide from them. They teach us that joy is found in both work and play.

Together the four suits of the Minor Arcana, create the areas of our existence needed to continue on the higher path. Following the wisdom of the actual path or the Major Arcana, we can utilize the aspects of our behavior or the Minor Arcana to create the endurance and focus to complete the journey.

Your journey through the twenty-two steps will be a pleasant one complete with everything you ever desired. The following is your personal road map.

MAJOR ARCANA

SPECIAL FEATURES

Each Major Arcana has a meaning for different aspects of your life. Here is a brief explanation of the categories found at the end of each Major Arcana.

ruler   each card has a planetary influence. As we interact with the cosmic features of planets and their signs each bears a special influence on our actions.

colors   color, like sound and scents, have living vibrations. They will influence our mental, physical and spiritual well-being.

essence   aromatherapy is the science of how scents affect us. Essential oils (make sure they are natural and not synthetic) may have positive results. Scents may be worn, used in baths or in other ways.

activities   each card carries with it a series of physical actions that may shape and explain the meaning of the card.

occupations   it just may help to know where our natural talents can be focused.

role in life   as we travel the path our purpose may change. Here is a description of where we are at the present moment

cautions   what are the pitfalls? What are the actions to avoid?

major issue   this is the central theme of each card

inner feeling   this is an explanation of the inner personality of each Major Arcana *love interest*   the natural way the personality interacts with a romantic partner

residence   this may be the environment best suited for the personality

trips   if and when you travel, this may help you to have a better trip.

family   how does this personality relate in the family structure

health   each card carries with it a series of health indicators

finances   what is the best way to obtain success

to do   how can you complete the lessons of this card

day of the week   there is a favorable influence on this day for the activity you have in mind

expression   use this as an affirmation. Write it down, repeat it to yourself, over and over. It really works.

THE FOOL

0

The Fool represents the beginning of the journey. It is time to set out on your own for the discovery of new territories. The Fool holds the potential for moving past hopeless feelings of despair. While he has a dual meaning, both can be valuable in preparing us for the journey ahead. On the one hand, if it were not for the Fool, there would be no journey. On the other hand, the Fool warns us to be careful. Without the Fool, there would be no risk taking. In fact, you would not be reading this book if you had not decided to take a risk. In all we know of the logical process, there is still something missing. It is the inner fire that has at some time burned in each and every one of us. This is the inner curiosity and potential wonderment preceding the voyage. The Fool has decided not to play it safe. He has decided to trust the favors of nature and move forward. Perhaps this relates to a relationship, business decision, or health issue.

Since he is called the Fool, it can be assumed that his trip is not well thought out, that those who think this are indeed the real fools. For he has in his innocent wisdom decided that the purpose of the trip is to gain knowledge as he moves along. One valuable lesson of the Fool is to

never assume. If you do not have any information that tells the story, then it may be best to simply acknowledge that you *don't know*. It is not a fool who admits what they do not know. It is a fool who pretends to know something when they really do not. The Fool uses the natural elements. God sent inspiration and his inner desire to guide him.

In this card, the bright yellow background lets us realize the possibilities of gathering knowledge and information along the way. The Fool seems to be taking a breath of fresh air in the wide open space. In one hand he has a white rose, a symbol of innocence and purity. In the other hand he has a wand and a wallet containing all he needs to make his journey. His faithful companion will be a constant reminder of his faith and self confidence. His sleeves blow in the wind as he seeks the next direction his travels will take him. His boots are made for quick and expedient travel. Through all his travels the sun continues to shine down upon him. He is carefree and carries no extra worries with him.

The Fool is a whimsical character who carries the potential for great achievements. He remains ready to heed the call of the wild. He has trust in his inner self and fears nothing. While he does not have the physical courage of the Strength or the Emperor's force, he has a power of equal measure. It is the God force in each of us. It is the spirit of freedom and growth available when we need it. He represents the ability to break free from restrictions and create a new possibility.

Positive Meaning—Mystical, enchanting, whimsical. The beginning of a creative adventure. Inspiration from above. Be wise before you decide to make a decision. Prepare for a change, it is on the way. Everyone must take risks at some point. It is time to develop new ways of doing things. Fly with the wind. Have faith in yourself. God is on your side, if your cause is pure and just. Lucky you! Pray, meditate, then go for it. Movement, change, fresh air. Money will come to you soon. Choose between good or evil. Visions and dreams. Courage and charm will help you achieve your goals.

Detriment—Get all the facts first. Do not assume. Someone refuses to listen to good advice. You are carrying too much baggage. Get rid of what no longer does you any good. There is a need to loosen up and be free of sadness. Not the best time to start something new. Get in touch with God through prayer and faith. A journey will be delayed. Someone may attempt to cheat or misuse someone or something.

Special Features

ruler   air

color   crystal, transparent, clear

essence   peppermint, eucalyptus, menthols

activities   movement, travel, change

occupations   sales people, workshop leaders, philosophers, world travelers, pioneers, explorers, scientists, healers, media, television, and radio

role in life   to explore the unknown

caution   never assume

major issue   new direction, beginning of a journey or relationship

inner feeling   courage, excitement, wonder

love interest   nature and natural wonders

residence   new environment or time to purchase something new for the home

trips   travel to a new location for a visit

family   resolve old conflicts and start on a new foot

health   problems with stress and patience

finances   success comes from making a change

to do   plan, investigate, and look before you leap. But do, by all means, leap

day of week   everyday

expression   It is in the light of God that I feel protection and inspiration. I will seek out all that is wonderful and exciting as I gain insight and meaning to highlight my inner being.

THE MAGICIAN

1

With one hand pointed up toward the sky and the other hand pointed down, the Magician no doubt represents the unity of heaven and earth. As the story goes, it is the messenger from God who travels from heaven to earth with a message for human kind. The Magician is a messenger. He initiates the beginnings of all things by bringing them together. This is the message of individual and world harmony. Between heaven and earth there is air. Through the air, messages of communications travel. Voice, music, television and radio waves, and other forms of expression need his vehicle for their expression.

In front of him he has gathered the four universal elements—cups (water), swords (air), wands (fire), and pentacles (earth). It is with the understanding of how each of these forces work that he will begin to synergize his message into reality. He stands waiting for others to hear his message and begin the process of manifestation. It is through the understanding and harmonizing of nature's forces that we will proliferate and progress. He has made the decision to apply his great skill and knowledge for the benefit of human kind. When properly blended together the four elements will create the answers to all his desires. However, keep in mind that the key is to properly blend them. Each force must be balanced, tested, and mixed to the proper proportion. Too much fire will cause the project or relationship to overheat. Too much emotion or water will cause it to drown, while too much air will not allow it to establish a foundation, and too much earth will not allow it the flexibility it needs.

It is not the task of the Magician to make it work. His job is to gather the elements and inform the participants of their existence. He

THE MAGICIAN.

is after all the messenger of God. Although he does have great power and knowledge of the magical arts he has chosen not to use them at this time, perhaps recognizing that there is still more work to do. The Magician represents new beginnings. He is an initiator. He can get things in motion through his communication skills. As a practical person he teaches us to add meaning and purpose to what we do. Perhaps his hands point the direction we must take to fulfill our goals. They can also represent our dual natures. One hand representing hope, faith, and positive thinking, and the other representing doubt, fear, and negative thinking. In order to create a new beginning, the past must be let go. This seems to be a recurring theme in the tarot. Remember—What is past has passed, and it won't come back.

Indeed, the Magician tells us not to abandon our faith, but to stay in touch with the higher forces and our inner beliefs. The aura around him is bright, and the yellow background suggests his great mental abilities. With such intellectual capacity, he can accomplish just about anything he sets his mind to. He must, however, remember to stay in balance. He must also remember his purpose and mission. For his powers to work, all phases of his life must be in order. Now that the decision has been made to re-enter the world of practicality, or begin a new relationship, or start a new career, forces indicate it is time to start. It is time to commit to the process with no hesitations.

His white garment is covered with a red robe. This indicates both his innocence and his courage. The Magician is not afraid to move on, to explore the new. As he has recently returned from the folly of the

Fool, he is rejuvenated and energized, ready to put his vast knowledge to the proper use. The Magician still waits for the right moment and the right people before the process can begin. Once they begin, the concept of synergy, mixing together, or alchemy, will be a successful one.

Making this conscious decision to return to the fold or try it one more time is not an easy one for us. It requires courage and innocence. Hopefully we have wiped the slate clean of past hurts, and disappointments.

To make it work, we must also apply discipline and fortitude. The journey may be a long one. The results however will be favorable providing we can apply our skill, patience, and courage to the situation. One of the main tasks of the Magician is to bring things together. While the Magician has the capacity to be a healer he awaits the person who dedicates their life to this profession as a specialist. He also has the capacity for business, the arts, sciences, and philosophy. Instead he chooses to continue on the path as a messenger bringing together people, places, and things.

He says, "The time is now for you to do it. Stop procrastinating." The power of the Magician must be used wisely. If it is abused it will backfire and work against you. The querist is warned against deceit, trickery, and manipulating schemes. You are advised to stay on the path of light and never venture into the darkness. Get-rich-quick schemes are not advised, just as revenge, gossip, and unjust criticism are ill advised.

The Magician is a light worker. The flowers that surround him are in full bloom. If you observe closely, you will notice that the flowers above are reaching toward the earth, and the flowers below are reaching to the heavens—symbolic of the need for consolidation and unity in all things.

The Magician is quite a person. The lessons are powerful and accurate. His ability to communicate is exceptional. He is organized, skillful, original, confident, quick, and creative.

Positive Meaning—Communication will be received or sent. Use the proper timing and execution in all communications. The time is now. Inspiration from the higher ideals. Success in written projects. Mass communication—television, radio, film, speech and newspapers are indicated. Communicate what you desire, you can achieve it. New beginnings approaching. Use communication to help, not to hurt or get something for nothing. Now is a good time to send messages to loved ones, co-workers or family. Make calls or send correspondence. Ability to pull together abstract ideas and structure them for a meaningful purpose. Contact a loved one. Be decisive. Communicate from your inner self, not superficially. Recognize your true powers within. Use willpower and mental energy. Use patience and start at the proper time. Be courageous and go for it.

Detriment—Communication is not clearly thought out. Sending or receiving mixed messages. Not using true skills for higher purpose. Speech impediment. Breathing or lung difficulties. Need to organize and gather more facts before deciding. Indecision regarding romance, family, or career. Need to be more practical. Consider all options. If traveling, consider all obstacles. Being too superficial or insincere. Trickery, deceit, or manipulation is involved. Need to expand consciousness. Hold off on new beginnings until more information is available. Need to recheck financial figures, leases, or contracts. Need to harmonize with family, friends, and co-workers. Lacking courage and will. Need to focus. Energies are scattered.

Special Features

ruler   mercury
color   yellow, grey
essence   amber, sage, eucalyptus, lavender, peppermint, lilac
occupations   writer, t.v., radio, media, reporter, advertising, lecturer, teacher, student, merchant, business, editor, publishing
role in life   communicator, messenger, bearer of information
cautions   be patient, honest, straightforward. Be aware of theft, and deceit. Get to the point. Stay focused on one goal at a time.
major issue   need to see, hear, or say something important
inner feelings   innate wisdom. "I know it all."
love interest   mental and intellectual associations
home   near clean air or use air purifiers or filters
trips   by air or train

•

career　　many choices, choose wisely

health　　problems associated with arms, hands, movement, lungs, teeth, and nervous disorders

finances　　great potential

day of the week　　Wednesday

expression　　I have the capacity to communicate with others. I will use this power for the benefit of others and for my growth and total awareness.

THE HIGH PRIESTESS

2

The High Priestess represents the power of our inner self. We are often unaware of our deeper powers—the intuitive part of ourselves that has gathered information throughout our lifetime. At the heart of all being is a cosmic force which makes the world go around. It touches and influences every aspect of our lives. So too is the reflection of the moon, ruler of the High Priestess. There she sits, in confidence, but still showing the eagerness for new knowledge. The High Priestess is surrounded by an aura of mystery. She poses with what might be described as austere wisdom. In her lesson live the possibilities of inner discovery. Spirituality, wisdom, and meditation are some of her traits. Through the organization of our skills (also the task of the Magician) the High Priestess sits in contemplation, observing the results of their synergy. She will take what the Magician has gathered and start some action. Her task is results or manifestation. The High Priestess is confident, and offers inspiration to the querist. She encourages others to experience her search for inner knowledge. Knowledge about one's self. The High Priestess is secure with her femininity and uses this power to achieve her end results. She has released the past and is very aware of the strength contained in the intuitive abilities.

The High Priestess is associated with the Egyptian goddess called Isis. As the goddess of fertility, Isis offered her wisdom and knowledge to the god Osiris.

Her number is two. This represents unions, connections, and the

THE HIGH PRIESTESS

unity of opposites. The opposites of hot and cold, day and night, and most importantly, the conscious and the subconscious. In her valuable lesson we are taught the importance of harmony and balance. Before any relationship or project can achieve success, it must be complete. To maintain harmony and balance, opposites must reach a resolution. This often means that we must love with a pure love, instead of a superficial love. We must be sincere and look at all sides of a situation.

It is because of her sensitivity that the High Priestess is able to perceive the needs and desires of others.

The High Priestess rules over families and relatives. She is gentle yet strong, confident yet humble, reflective yet forceful. She has great insight, and leans toward psychic abilities. She is nurturing, emotional, and changeable.

The High Priestess teaches us to focus inward. To meditate and utilize our silent powers. She teaches us to change the inside and then watch as the outside changes. Her knowledge is from an ancient source, yet she remains open to new guidance. Her trait of independence accompanies her giving nature. Inspiration and creativity come naturally to her. While she can heal the wounds of others, she will retreat into her shell if she senses danger. Her deep sense of caring and nurturing often leave her in need of rest and rejuvenation. She is usually giving more than she is receiving, and must rely on her inner strength to pull her through. When this card is a part of your selection it hints at the need to reflect inwardly for solutions. Perhaps even the need to take a walk around a monastery, visit a resort, retreat, or take a walk by the seashore. Even a peaceful walk along a babbling brook may be just what you need.

As she sits between two pillars of opposite color, the High Priestess demonstrates the need for unity and balance in all things. Unlike the Justice who balances two issues, the High Priestess will blend them together. This is very much like the yin/yang sign of harmony, where you see a small bit of yang contained in the yin and a small bit of yin contained in the yang. In every masculine energy, there are feminine energies. Likewise, in each female energy there are masculine energies. In her hand she holds the scroll of the hidden mysteries—the secret document of wisdom. On her chest she wears the sign of the cross, indicating her universal nature, and the ability to understand the natural forces of the universe. In a sense, a part of the scroll is guarded or hidden. She will offer it, but not to just anyone. There is a hidden force or potential in each of us. It is through the lessons of the High Priestess that we will have the introspection to locate and bring forth these powers. In the background you will notice the fruit of life, indicating her powers of fertility. Yellow and red symbolize the blending of both intellectual and physical energy. Her blue robe and headdress let us know that, for the most part, she has accepted her role and is at peace with herself.

Perhaps one of the most beautiful natural sights in the sky is the crescent moon. In this case it lies at her feet denoting her connection with the changes in the moon. The yellow background of the Magician has created a base for the High Priestess to place her throne. Notice the color of her floor. On her head is another phase of the moon, the full moon. She is desired by men as the perfect wife, partner, and confidant.

Each of us has a deep and hidden secret. It is like a skeleton we keep in our closet. Through the lessons of the High Priestess, we will learn to let go of the fear attached to this secret. These secrets may cause us to withdraw, or even consider a project hopeless. Nothing should be hopeless just because of a silly mistake we made in the past. The hidden scroll teaches us the need to remove the fear, confront the secret, and move on with our lives. Remember, the person next to you has a secret as confining as your secret. Why hide the truth? Confront it, accept it, and move on. This can be done through self reliance, self discovery, and meditation. As the moon represents the reflective side of our personalities, the High Priestess represents negotiation instead of war, sensitivity versus harshness, unity over discord, and loyalty in place of unfaithfulness.

Positive Meaning—Be open to the wisdom of ancient teachings. Integrate the mistakes of the past into the plans of the future by not repeating them. Do not fear the feminine principle. Start a new project at the new moon. Meditate on it for answers during the full moon. Know your true self. Establish a regular rhythm for success. Movement, growth, fertility. Luck in this project. Delicate issue, approach with sensitivity and kindness for best results. Emotional relationship. Need to see inside of the issue instead of on the surface. Choose partners carefully. Learn discrimination. Throw away junk or unwanted items. Do not disclose all at this time. Keep a secret. Be flexible, flow with the change, it is for the better. Be charming. Stay focused. Public affairs, politics, organizations, leadership. Silence is golden. Pay greater attention to the home and your family. Time to start both. Acquire more techniques to make something work. Learn to use the power of your sight, hearing, taste, touch, and smell. Be subtle, and gentle. Do not confuse sexual with sensual. Success comes through involvement with family and loved ones, or best friends. Keep your spiritual beliefs to yourself, until someone shows they are ready for them. Begin creative projects. You will have peace, harmony, and beauty in your life soon. Things in pairs. Focus on creative projects rather than intellectual ones at this time. Be independent but co-operative. May need to teach or do further study. Above all trust your inner feelings and intuition. Stay focused on your inner desires, wants and needs. There is still more work to do.

Detriment—Loss of self worth. Too moody. Keep emotions in check. Health problems in chest area. Needs more confidence. Not a good time to travel. Need stable home environment. Fear, anger, and doubt cause problems. Do not be too trusting. Keep secrets for a while longer. Visit a church, temple, mosque, or sanctuary for inspiration. Finances uncertain at this time. Listen to soothing music, especially violin or harp music. Being too mysterious, or in a shell too long. Shy, unstable, untrustworthy, critical. Too much idle time. Emotions may cause health problems. Be more discriminating instead of staying in seclusion. Need to balance logic and intuition. Spending too much time at home. Get out and see the world. Believe in your natural skills. Too much technique. Being too harsh, or insensitive.

Special Features

ruler   moon

color   white, silver

essence   gardenia, lemon, lotus, myrrh, sandalwood

occupations   psychic, business person, teacher, parent, spiritual teacher, leader, planner, antique collector, water sports, navigator, import-export, work with children

role in life   teach the wisdom of inner knowledge and self reflection. Impart true love and sensitivity.

cautions   do not be too sensitive or retreat into a shell. Let go of the past.

major issue   secrets, hidden facts, hidden potential, inner wisdom, intuition, ancient wisdom, family

love interest   emotional bonds, deep caring, attachments

residence   near water, move in May, June, or July

inner feelings   realization at the deepest levels

trips   travel with a mate

family   be more sensitive and less secretive

health   be aware of problems in breasts, chest, stomach, bladder, and with all fluids. Drink more water.

finances   success with home-based businesses, mail order, family activities. General outlook is good. Take a chance.

day of the week   Monday

expression   I enjoy the beauty of harmony and the inner workings of the universe. They provide the guidance for all wisdom.

THE EMPRESS

3

The Empress exemplifies the love we all seek. She is the mani-

festation of self-love, individual love, love of nature, love for the family, and of course love for a lover.

She is known as the earth mother. As the High Priestess maintains many of her emotions internally, the Empress is the outward vehicle for the expression of those emotions. She is the goddess of Love, Harmony and Beauty. The Empress is the representation of Venus, with all the traits of a Venusian beauty. Some have referred to her as Aphrodite. She is expansive, attractive, and likes to have what she describes as the finer things in life.

There is a valuable lesson to be learned through our association with the Empress. It is that of love. Not just the conversation of love, but the higher principle of loving. The act of showing love, and meaning it. Even if it is only for the moment.

As the High Priestess has taken the tools of the Magician for intuitive contemplation, the Empress prefers to spend her time acting. She is earth bound and should surround herself with the joys of nature. Her concern for the most part is within the material world. She chooses interaction and partnership over isolation, although she can at a moment's notice leave a situation, never to return.

Through the Empress we learn that receiving love means we should be willing to give love. As many people do, the Empress, in her exalted state, does not fear love or being in love. In fact, she thrives on love. There is a difference between the superficial acts of pretending and real love. The Empress will show us the difference. She will show us how to love.

As she begins with her love of nature, she reaches to brighten humanity with her elegance and artistic sense. Often she is confused about her true purpose and spends time giving where she is taken for granted. Her rewards are then minimal, but she picks her heart up and moves on to try again, always seeking the meaning of the perfect love.

The Empress may mean a man or woman in the artistic fields of music, dance, painting, fashion, or theater. These are the places that artistic beauty may be best exemplified. Don't tell that to the Empress however. She will find beauty wherever she goes. If it is not there when she arrives, it will be there by the time she leaves. More times than not, she wears her heart on her chest, letting people know just who she is, and why she is there.

Unless the Empress has learned the lessons ahead of her, she may also abuse her gifts, by turning on the charm. A fisherman's net for the person who finds her female passions irresistible. For the most part, the Empress is kind, caring, considerate, and highly productive. She is fertile and represents the nurturing attributes of the mother hen. She enjoys pleasure, and uses her senses for that purpose. Perfumes, fine clothes, expensive furniture, and lovely surroundings will suit her taste.

The Empress has many needs of her own. The greatest is the need to be and feel loved. She will often go out of her way to achieve these goals. In some cases the love she gives is never returned. Usually, she expects it to be so. While the High Priestess shares unconditionally, the Empress does have conditions. If that is not enough, she will present terms along with those conditions.

Her bright, happy energy makes things fertile. She knows the meaning of new beginnings, as well as she knows the meaning of false starts.

Harmony is a key word to this elegant lady. Harmony in all things. Both universal and personal harmony. Once she has reached the understanding of her purpose and the realm of her true womanhood, she will obtain her harmony. For it is then that she feels really alive and well.

Like her friend and confidante, the High Priestess, the Empress occupies a throne. Her's is the throne of rulership. She is in control, and likes to be in control. As she is happiest as wife to the Emperor, she will not hesitate to assume his role if he fails to meet his obligations. She is the power behind the throne, who has chosen to be advisor, wife, mother, and keeper of the peace.

The Empress wears a long flowing robe with the symbol of flowers as a design. Seated on a cushion atop of her seat she is a lover of comfort and the easy life. To her right is a heart with the emblem of the woman inscribed. She is of course surrounded by nature, with flowers, trees, water and fresh air. Now we notice that the yellow floor of the High Priestess is behind and above her head. The conscious mind is now in manifestation, active and forever doing something. In her hand she holds a scepter with which she will create something. On her head is a crown with twelve stars. One for each month, as she constantly renews her energy.

Around her neck we notice the pearls of wisdom. She sits, poised and elegant, awaiting the love she seeks.

Within the aspects of the Empress we will find the essence of all things. The beginning and the end. She will help put our thoughts into action.

Positive Meaning—Fertility, beauty, love. A need to understand the concept of love. A satisfactory relationship is coming soon. Abundance in all things. Fortune and luck will come through relationships. Three days, three weeks, or three years. Trinity, pyramids. You must do something at least three times for it to work. Person in the arts. Relationship based on mutual love. True love. Sit tight and be patient. Issues of the heart. Abundance is coming. Pregnancy, or child to be born. Female, mother, sister, daughter. Linking mental, physical, and emotional energy. Wife to the Emperor. Goddess of love, beauty, harmony. Need to be around nature, to give love, and to receive love. Trust in love. Love yourself more. Express your true feelings to someone. A good card with many positive outcomes. Follow your true heart. Plant seeds for your future. Cosmetics, fashion, beauty, new furniture, new home. Natural foods will help keep you in harmony and good health. Need to accept the responsibility of motherhood or leadership. Work behind the scenes. Be more expansive. Visit a beauty salon. People born April 19th-May 19th or September 23rd-October 23rd.

Detriment—Being selfish, and sexually manipulative. Withholding love. Delay. Infertility. Need for better diet, stress management, or spiritual rejuvenation. Outcome will be delayed at this time. This may not work out as expected. Being too thrifty. Not expansive enough. Flirtatious, disloyal, jealous. Need to nurture the feminine part of your personality. Need creative outlet. Life is out of balance. Change the way you do things. Purchase something to lift your spirits. A long delay. Love will not be returned. Be more discriminating. Pleasure, joy and happiness may be delayed. Be more mature about the issue. Need to take more initiative. Add to wardrobe. Fear in expressing true feelings.

Special Features

ruler   venus

color   emerald green, rose, yellow

essence   rose, all flowers, strawberry

activities   assimilation of information, feelings, and actions

occupations   artists, dance, music, florists, decorators, receptionists, leaders, architects, beauty consultants, designers, jewelers

role in life   give and receive love. Manifest creative projects. Give and receive support from Emperor.

cautions   never attempt to force or pull love from someone. Let it happen naturally. Provide pleasure and beauty for self as well as others.

major issue   beauty, harmony, balance and wisdom.

inner feelings   need for love, and partnership. Resolve past hurts. They are obstacles.

love interest   nurturing Love is the basis. Exchange of feelings.

residence   natural surroundings, with flowers, trees, and birds.

trips   to meadows, flower gardens, or museums

family   release hostilities involving, mother, sister, or daughter

health   problems in throat, kidneys, lumbar region

finances   abundance, success through partnerships and unions

to do   give love to receive love. Make the proper choices or disappointments in love will occur.

day of week   Friday

expression   love makes the world go around. I will allow it to come into my life as I release the past and look forward to the future.

THE EMPEROR

4

The Emperor represents masculine energy. He is the part of us that takes responsibility and sets out to reach new heights. To list the Emperor's traits we would say he has courage, power, and is a good leader.

When you select this card you are or will be facing a decision which will require assertiveness and sensitivity. As a leader the Emperor teaches us the importance of connecting wisdom and compassion to our decision making process. The Emperor is easy to anger and must constantly work to maintain inner harmony. It is the Emperor who establishes the guidelines for law and order. As he consults with his wife and partner, the Empress, he remembers the importance of abiding by the rules, especially if the job is to be completed.

Once again we should remember that the Emperor is a part of each of us (as are all the cards). No matter that it is a male card. It has valuable lessons that speak to the masculine side of our personalities. The Emperor recognizes the importance of the Empress and interacts with her accordingly. He has accepted his role as leader, and he is fair and just. His group relies on him to lead the way.

As with any good leader, the Emperor will make regular visits with his family, friends, or employees, to maintain a proper perspective on reality. He is most concerned with the material world. More so than the Magician or the High Priestess. It is in the material world that he finds his greatest challenges. When the Emperor carries forth the spirit of the magician and adds the wisdom of the Hermit he becomes a man of great power.

Often the symbol can represent men or women in the military. While they have a heart for the unknown and adventure, they are still conservative and traditional in their ways. They believe in following the established system. It is within the boundaries of what is well established that they will seek to chart new paths.

We often find the Emperor's personality among style setters, builders, and law makers. They take interest in reaching one step further than the last person. They will often be bold in dress, combining the traditional fashions with a new twist, such as a new way of wearing a belt, or a new hair style. Not that they are outrageous, but they are the first to be seen with the new fad.

The Emperor is the guide for what is right or wrong. He will dictate what we will, and will not, do. Trying new things is familiar to him. It is important for people with this personality to think before they act. Moving head-first into issues may often get them into predicaments where they must spend valuable time trying to get out. In general, their's is a rational, structured thought process. They can be counted on and are reliable. If they can integrate the feminine aspects of their personality, they will maintain both stability and poise when confronted with important issues. Courage, strength, and leadership come naturally. They will accept almost any challenge. Often the more difficult a task, the better it is for these people.

If you need a foundation on which to build an organization, seek a person with the traits of the Emperor. He can be spontaneous, energetic, and will eventually get the job done. They are tireless workers who know how to delegate. They are not afraid to speak their minds.

Through the Emperor we can learn the values of negotiation. It is not always necessary to argue, fuss, or fight to get results. He rules with a firm but resourceful hand. The Emperor is of royalty and feels it inside. He also represents sexual energy that is controlled. It is through the union with the Empress for procreation that he has learned to direct his vast sexual energy. Together they will sit on the throne as the heads of the family. Together they will balance the energy of one another. She, offering the wisdom and power of love, and he, contributing the essence of power, courage, and responsibility.

He is fond of manifestation and reality. He loves to build. The bigger the better. While others sit and procrastinate, he will take the initiative and start the job, then await the help of others whom he can trust to get the job finished. He is resourceful and makes as many friends as he does enemies. But whatever the outcome he usually maintains the respect of everyone. Some are made uneasy by his impulsive, brash style of doing things. Others become fearful of his almost military regimentation when it comes to his sense of survival. Emperors know how to take care of themselves and of others.

You will notice he is wearing a yellow crown. This reminds us to always think before we act. Two of the jewels on the crown are red, no doubt rubies, which symbolize energy, and activity. In his right hand he holds the Egyptian sign of the cross, the Ankh. It represents life, vitality and victory. In his left hand, he holds the globe of the world, as he constantly awaits the next place of his conquest. On the front of his throne are the head of the Ram. His sign, of course, is Aries, the ram.

Yet he wears the peaceful blue color as his undergarment. This will always remind him of the purpose he has been selected as the ruler or leader. It is to lead the way to material well-being and, ultimately, inner peace.

The sun lights up the right side of the card, but it does not illuminate the left. Eventually he will see the sun light up the entire sky. At the moment it waits dormant for him to complete his process. His white beard lets us know he is older now and more mature. He also has innocent and pure intentions.

Action is his claim to fame. The fire burns day and night. Through our involvement with the Emperor we will learn not to procrastinate. To get to it, to move on it...*Now.* He will often seek solitude to regroup from the long, perilous journey. It is during this time the Emperor will search his globe and begin to create the next adventure. They are the first in line. At the head of the class. They will quickly climb the corporate ladder. If they can remember the important lessons of the Empress, they more than likely move even faster and farther.

The Emperor can have a fiery temperament when it comes to competition. They are ambitious, and spirited. True, they may fall out at the end of the day, but no one will ever know it. The Emperor was born to be a leader. He is comfortable giving orders, and must be sure to not be too bossy. The Emperor is independent, but finds purpose in the many people who come in and out of his life.

Positive meaning—Create or build a foundation. Be compassionate as well as strong in your leadership. Confirm the facts before you do it. A question of reliability. Seek positive people who understand you. Finish the job before moving on to a new one. Start a business of your own. Success love or romance with an Aries person. Yes, you may now start issues with the law, or rules and regulations. The time will be four weeks, four days, or four months. You need four of something, or it will happen in April. Pay more attention to your health, especially headaches or nervous tension. There is nothing to fear, be courageous. A new gift is coming to you soon. Accept it, and thank the sender. Take more control for results. Start now to build. A male has a hand in your future. He is a strong willed person, and may be aggressive. Issue with father, husband, or son.

Detriment—You are being too aggressive, learn to control your temper. Be patient, now is not the time to move or start something new. Ask more questions, get more details. You are being dominated by something or someone. You are exercising too much control. Let go of something or someone in your life who is causing you undue tension. You must break the bonds, and become more independent. You are doubtful about what is right or what is wrong. You are procrastinating and calling it cautious action. Too impulsive, slow down and anchor. Learn to work with others for best results.

Special Features

ruler	Aries
color	red, crimson
essence	frankincense, cinnamon, allspice, ginger
activities	action, sex, courage, passion
occupations	inspirational speakers, corporate executives, personal trainers, administrative assistants, builders, construction workers, photographers, manufacturers, military, typists, all athletes

role in life   to inspire and motivate, by establishing examples of leadership and courage

cautions   headstrong, too bossy, get all the facts before setting things into motion

major issue   begin new projects, put ideas into concrete form

inner feelings   easy to anger, control, responsible

love interest   mate who gets results, passionate relationship

residence   places where there is activity, or the mountains

trips   travel to new and exciting locations

family   resolve issues with father, brother, husband, or son

health   accident prone, headaches, or back problems

to do   get in touch with the compassionate, part of your inner self for balance. Learn to forgive and forget.

day of week   Tuesday

expression   I possess the courage and wisdom to start what I may conceive. I motivate and inspire others to achieve more.

Be a constructive leader.

THE HIEROPHANT

5

The Hierophant represents the manifestation of the higher principles in the universe. It is the task of the Hierophant to see the practicality in all things. This is the way to manifest them, taking them from the stage of spiritual thoughts into real form. He is the priest, the counselor, or the religious person who exercises their faith in or out of church. Where the Emperor is the commander and the lawmaker, the Hierophant gives us the personal right to obey or disobey the law. The law is already inscribed when he appears. It is he who shall give interpretation and show the need for such a law. The Emperor, in his job as leader, does not have the time nor the patience to show us why these laws are necessary. Nor is he totally focused on the universal laws as much as he is focused on the laws of society. The Hierophant is concerned with the higher laws. In fact, morals, integrity, and principles

THE HIEROPHANT

concern him most. Too often he will become enticed with the traditional or orthodox aspects of religion and even become dogmatic in his belief. For the most part, he too lives in the material world, manifesting the creations of others, making them real and tangible.

The lessons of the Hierophant will show us to have faith in the higher powers. They do indeed exist, and are ever present in our lives. As we face the doubt of our true convictions, perhaps are about to stray from the path, the Hierophant will provide a tangible sign that victory is near. He will point ouf the value of morality, in church as well as outside of church.

To some the laws of religion and of the church have only surface meaning. The Hierophant takes these laws to heart. He not only knows the meaning, but gives them purpose in everyday life. For the most part, he is a practical person. A person of common sense. He will plan, step by step, and then move when he is good and ready. The true depth of the Hierophant's lesson lies in the purpose as opposed to the result. His purpose lies in the higher values and ideals. The result is manifestation on the earthly plane, in the material world.

Like the Empress the Hierophant has loving vibrations that produce charm and sensuality. Love of God, love of good, and love of self, are lessons this step on the path share with us.

We see, by meditating on the Hierophant card, he wears a crown of intellect. It is not simply mental activity, but the brilliant pronunciation of the holy spirit in thought.

There are several layers to the crown, each being a step closer to the God consciousness. There are three crosses over his robe and one on each shoe, each displaying his dedication to the elements of the earth. Covering his throat is the blue color of peace and tranquility. Since it covers his throat, we may hear his words of dedication and acknowledge his ability to sing the praises of the higher values. He is also a musical person, who can send healing vibrations from his voice.

As does the High Priestess, the Hierophant sits between two pillars demonstrating the central tarot theme of yin/yang, good/bad, male/female. The theme of opposites, and the need for balance in all things. Before him are two students, or seekers of the higher ideals. He holds his right hand up displaying the inspiration he continually imparts. In his left hand he holds a staff with three levels—mind, body, and spirit. In front of him are the keys to the universe. No doubt they show the need for knowledge and clear thinking. Notice, one student, or monk, wears red, and one wears blue. What does this mean to you?

His robe is a bright red, reflecting that he is an active person, who reveres in physical energy.

The Hierophant is a family person. As with all the Major Arcana, this card can represent energy in a man or a woman. He faces a constant test of his faith. Situations that require faith confront him daily. After all, he is only human. The question will arise, "What should I do...give up or go on? Should I take the easy way out, or should I continue with morality and integrity?" It is through the Hierophant that we learn to blend the spiritual with the practical.

The Hierophant constantly faces challenges. He is practical and self reliant. Patience is a mainstay of this ability. It is through patience that we develop the will to continue against all odds. Waiting is sometimes a key factor in watching the seeds mature for harvest. The Hierophant uses the tools of the material world. He understands the purpose of money, clothing, shelter, and insurance funds.

Persons born April 21-May 22 are confronted with these values. Or this may mean this time period will be important to you. The Hierophant can be slow to anger. However, once he is angered, watch out for the charging bull who knows no limitations.

Although the struggle is not as tedious as that of the Devil, or the Hermit, the Hierophant, faces many obstacles. Perhaps this is why they must develop the patience and grounding to endure and maintain faith in the higher principles. It takes him a long time to gain the answers, but once he has them, neither heaven nor earth can change his mind. This is true faith.

Positive Meaning—You are on a solid foundation. You may now begin. Trustworthy, honest individual. You can overcome all obstacles with patience, faith, and fortitude. A taskmaster. The religious side of a person. Traditional religion. Loyal, individual. Time to start a family. Trust your inner self. You must convert your spiritual values into material well-being. Money, banks, and material possessions. You will face obstacles, but can work through them. Make a commitment. Resolve family issues at this time. A Taurus person figures in the picture. Teacher, student. Do some research. Meditate. Music, singing, speech. Success in legal matters, or contracts. Apply spiritual knowledge, it can work for you. Hold out for the best—when it arrives, it will come fast. Religions, laws, and conservative issues.

Detriment—Self indulgence, and stubbornness. Disloyal and dishonest. Double check all contracts. Do not be bull headed. Do not gamble at this time. Go for the sure thing. Do not make a change now, wait for a better situation. You are moving too slow, make up your mind and start planning. You have lost your faith. Overweight, because of overindulgence of refined food and drink. Let go. You are too superstitious. Be more practical with your spiritual beliefs. Not conforming to society or regulations. Look for the higher meaning in everything you do. You are trapped by your material and sexual desires.

Special Features

ruler   Taurus
color   pastels, pink, orange, blue
essence   magnolia, cherry, violet, rose
activities transform spirit into material
occupations   singers, bankers, accountants, farmers, sales, managers, superintendents, treasurers, artists, priests, spiritual leaders
role in life   maintenance of the status quo, conservation of law and order, and display of moral values
cautions   stubborn, dogmatic, lazy

major issue   teach and learn moderation in all things, rituals, and observation of higher ideals

inner feelings   joy and pleasure

love interest   passionate and sensual relationships

residence   meadows, near daffodils and butterflies

trips   overland by car, to experience the sights

family   good parent, and loyal child

health   problems in throat, voice, and neck

finances   the road to wealth is a long but sure one

to do   endure, be patient, keep the inner faith

day of the week   Friday

expression   When I continue to grow through overcoming all obstacles, I will experience the glory of God by my side. In this glory, all desires and wishes will manifest.

THE LOVERS

6

Here we have the representation of all relationships. The relationship of lovers, the relationship of the conscious and the subconscious, and the relationship of right and wrong. In these relationships we are given choices. Whenever two opposites resolve their differences to form a unity, a powerful connection is made. It means that all resistance is eliminated and progress can move straight ahead.

The Lovers represent pairs who have decided to become one. This can be husband and wife, boyfriend and girlfriend, employee and a job, or the male and female sides in each of us. As we attempt to make choices in our lives, we remain faced with making the right decisions. What exactly are the right decisions?

Through the lesson of the Lovers we are constantly encouraged to select good over evil, love over hate and harmony over disunity. The Lovers are the force that unify us for the satisfaction of our real desires.

It is often through this unity that we are able to see and understand more about our inner and outer personalities. The Lovers can mean a side of us that we have refused to recognize. Such as a repressed

THE LOVERS.

talent or skill. According to the Lovers it is time to allow that hidden element to surface.

For relationships to work, they require attention and nourishment. Not to mention co-operation and commitment. The Lovers remind us that half-commitment will bring half-results. Total commitment to whatever we do will bring us total results. There are always decisions to be made. Making them is a part of getting results.

If the Lovers appears in your spread, you should consider making a firm commitment to something or let it go. Superficial actions are not getting results and everybody is waiting for the other person to make the first move. To make any relationship work, time and space must be allocated to each participant for personal evaluation. This space may be in the form of a temporary separation, a change of location, or a vacation. The Lovers can apply to any relationships. There are many that we form throughout our lives.

Also it is The Lovers which remind us to constantly take a look at ourselves. Not just a look on the surface, but a deep look—a look into our motivations, feelings and attitudes.

In this card there is much joy. You will notice the brilliant sun spreading light and cosmic energy from above. Then there is the angel who carries the message of unity and blessing to the man and woman below. The angel has both hands raised and approves of the unity of the two elements. It is a spiritual message, as denoted by the purple garment. At the same time it is a union of two great minds who see eye to eye. Both people are nude, and have expressed their true nature to one another. Their relationship has physical connections. While the female energy looks to the angel, as if she was looking for a sign, the male energy keeps his attention focused on the female. Both have palms open and are receptive to the new possibilities created by their union. This is an important key to the act of confirming a relationship. If one party refuses to commit or to trust, or to express their true feelings, it will not work.

Communication is essential. Behind the female energy is the tree of life, with four pieces of fruit. Each one represents one of the four basic elements. She is the High Priestess, and the Empress who seeks greater inspiration. Behind the male energy are twelve leaves. One for each aspect of the zodiac, and one for each month of the year. Also on the female tree is the moving snake, who warns of an oncoming temptation. Temptation is always near. It is only through the faith of the Hierophant that we will resist temptation and select the higher path over the lower path. Both have been offered. It is a decision we must make each day. There is a hidden part of each of us. Often it is one of the secrets held by the High Priestess. Through positive partnerships, and relationships, we can often find the motivation to explore these hidden talents and skills. Another aspect of the Lovers is that of the unity between the conscious and subconscious minds. It means to feel on the inside in harmony with what you are portraying through your actions. As opposed to saying one thing and feeling a different way, it is wiser for the querist to harmonize both. Why fool yourself? The lovers teaches us the need to be true to ourselves. Then we will be better able to maintain happy and fruitful relationships.

Good is good and evil is evil. Which one do you choose? The confidence of the Emperor and the Empress let us know that we can believe in ourselves and remain in control of our lives. Through the lovers we will be able to integrate the total aspects of our wants and needs. This card can mean two people, two jobs, two times, two days, or two personalities. One way or another there is a decision to be made.

Positive Meaning—Love will be blessed. A message concerning another person or situation will arrive soon. The merging of two previous opposite forces. Success in partnerships. Make commitments. A choice of some type is necessary now. Take space to look at the situation. Separate yourself to be able to see the temptation. Pain or pleasure. Evil or good. Unity of two things. Be more decisive. Learn the meaning of universal love. Stop focusing on yourself and pay more attention to the other person. Blend your personality with your true feelings. Search for the child-like qualities in yourself. Take a writing, speech, or communications class. Speak to someone about a situation. Express yourself. A question regarding superficial and real feelings. Commit or quit. Say yes, or no, and stick to it. People born May 21- June 21 may be involved. Business and pleasure can be combined.

Detriment—you cannot make up your mind. You have chosen to give in to temptation. Someone is hiding something. There will be a separation. Not a good time for a union. All the facts are not on the table. The true meaning of a situation is being hidden. Understand the other persons point of view. Energies are scattered and should be focused. Leave out the petty conversation and get to the point—the heart of the issue, not the surface appearance. A need to expand the concept of real love into a concept of universal love.

Special Features

ruler   Gemini
color   orange, blue, yellow
essence   peppermint, strawberry, neroli, lavender
activities   speaking, poetry, traveling
occupations   computer operators, writers, television person-alities, newscasters, speech therapists, mimes, scientists, thinkers, mechanics, librarians, teachers, messengers, bartenders, agents
role in life   to communicate true feelings at both the conscious and subconscious levels
cautions   don't move too quickly, or too indecisively
major issue   relationships, unification of opposites, making deci-sions between good and bad
inner feeling   life is a duality, there must be two of everything
love interest   learn to love at the deeper levels
residence   fresh air, breezy climate, home filled with books
trips   travel by air. Go to libraries, or to mountain tops

family　　learn true meaning of sharing and caring

health　　possible problems with nerves, and or lungs

finances　　money will come quickly and unexpectedly

day of the week　　Wednesday

expression　　I desire the harmony of loving relationships. Through mutual trust and commitment, co-operation will result in the synergy of all our ideals.

THE CHARIOT

7

The Chariot represents the ultimate potential for triumph and victory. It is the manifestation of our energy to conquer and move through all obstacles. The Chariot will show us the way to harness our intuitive powers for the production of our goals. As the Chariot driver, we must know when to exhibit aggressive actions and when to be passive. While the aggressive side of our personality demands what it wants, the passive side of our energy will wait patiently to receive it. There is power in both styles. The aggressive way simply makes a decision, and enforces the action to get up and go after it. On the other hand, passive behavior recognizes the power in personal attraction and relies on the energies which are drawn to it.

We need both types of energies. One to go out and get what we want, and the other to be open to what comes our way. The Chariot teaches how to balance these energies, neither being too aggressive, or too passive. There is a time and a place for both. They, like many other opposites, must work together in harmony for us to reach our true potential.

The Chariot driver will soon be or has already been in a heated race. It is important for the Chariot driver to stay in total control. He must know when to turn the Chariot, when to let the horses have free reign, and when to let it go. If he turns it too hard, it will turn over and get off course. If he cannot slow it down when it is necessary, he will run into another Chariot or some other obstacle. If he cannot let it go when the time is right, he will not be able to gain enough speed, and will certainly not win the race.

You will notice by looking closely at the Chariot several important symbols. Over the rider's head hangs a canopy or covering. On his head he is wearing an eight pointed star. This signifies his association with money, wealth, and illumination. It is designed with the stars of the heaven. A cosmic blessing that he will achieve victory. It is consistent with divine order that he participate in the race. On each side of him are pillars, four to be exact. As another recurring theme throughout the tarot, he must acknowledge the power of the natural forces — fire, water, earth, and air. Together they provide the energy, intuition, skill and know-how to achieve victory. He wears a suit of armor to protect his physical body from injury and illness, just as we must eat healthy foods, exercise, and resolve our emotional troubles. On each of his shoulders is the crescent moon which can provide illumination and beauty in our lives. In this case they offer him both intellect and intuition to make his journey a safe one. The staff of knowledge is in his right hand, pointing out the importance of knowing the right direction to take during the race. In the background is a brilliant yellow representing the joy of participating in the situation, and the satisfaction received once the victory is obtained. In front, the chariot is led by two Egyptian sphinxes, one black and one white. They are seemingly opposite, but upon further examination, we will see they have a unity of purpose. Each is wearing the same headdress. There are many other symbols in the Chariot card. See which ones you can identify, and explain.

To achieve victory, the Chariot must rest when he is not active.

This is a part of the preparation. Self-discipline and stability are two more traits represented by the Chariot. He must also learn to conquer his fears and negative emotions. The Chariot is the end of the first path. It is the triumph or victory. When we have drawn this card, a victory is ahead if we can heed the lessons of the Chariot. The Chariot is a traveler. He has acquired the means of transportation needed to take his journey. People born June 21-July 21 are represented by this card. They may be male or female. These individuals are generally nurturing, sensitive, and family oriented. They must learn or can teach us to get in touch with our inner spirits. To trust our intuition and make more decisions to take control of our lives. Be the boss of your own destiny. Take control and begin to do what you really want to do. You can be successful.

Positive Meaning—Victory is near. Triumph and conquest will be yours if you stay focused on your goal. You must make clear choices. Get more results. Come out of your shell and let the games begin. Success in climbing the career ladder. Stay in control. Self-discipline is the answer. You are a pioneer, be self reliant. Persons born June 21-July 21 may assist you. Home and family. Move or relocate at this time. A health issue will be overcome. Harness and focus your energies. With each victory, couple it with humility and grace. Travel is in store. A business deal is near. Balance action with rest and tranquility. Drive for success must be controlled. Let victory be your goal.

Detriment—Too much time alone. You fear the outcome of an issue. There are negative feelings involved. A health problem may result from over eating or excessive behavior. You need more confidence. Believe in yourself. A family issue is present. Not the right moment to start a new project. Rest may be indicated before moving ahead. Self centered, egotistical, and too ambitious. May be too focused on the material benefits of the project, rather than the spirit of the project itself. Someone has sacrificed spiritual goals for power and control. Out of balance. Prejudice, and discrimination is present. Find a new direction, too many obstacles for success. Let your spirit be your guide.

Special Features

ruler Cancer

color silver, iridescents, white

essence gardenia, lemon, lotus, myrhh

activities reflection, psychic abilities, home projects

occupations gardeners, psychic healers, historians, business leaders, organizational heads, real-estate agents, travel business, athletes, sea merchants, explorers, antique collectors

role in life apply spiritual knowledge to inform and nurture

cautions keep emotions in balance. Guard against absorbing negative emotions from others

major issue triumph, victory, travel, overcome obstacles

inner feeling high sensitivity to environment

love interest love of family and people in the group

residence country, or near the water

trips short fruitful journeys, with time to rejuvenate

family often the head of the household, family is first

health problems with stomach and digestive system

finances potential to gain through things connected with the present and future.

to do let go of the past

day of the week Monday

expression I will achieve victory in everything I do. To do so I will remain spiritually and physically balanced at all times.

STRENGTH

8

The Strength tarot card represents our inner fortitude, will, and determination. It is the display of courage and the wisdom that must accompany it. As the name implies, Strength may be physical, emotional, or spiritual. A balance of all three keeps us fit to meet any challenge head on.

While the Chariot refers to our outer will and ability to overcome external obstacles, the Strength card refers to our inner will and the ability to overcome our inner obstacles. This is the taming of the inner beast. The conquering of ego, and self-centered behavior. We learn from the Strength card the power of love and its results. It is through expression of the universal love reflected in the Empress that we find the connection to our feminine powers. As we cut through the false pride and the ego to find these feminine powers the Strength will provide the path for their expression. Not being afraid to love, and not being afraid to demonstrate this love are traits of the Strength card. Through spiritual courage, we will hold fast in our convictions and overcome all obstacles. Courage must be accompanied by wisdom, lest it be a trait of the Fool.

The Strength is a model for the passions and uncontrolled behavior of our primal instincts. It can speak to the animal nature we will often return to if we feel threatened. Or this behavior will often be shown through lust and uncontrolled sexual activities. They may lead to infidelity, or deceit. There is a lesson here concerning the balance of two forces. One force is our spiritual power. The other is our physical power. When the two unite and become one force our actions will become aligned with our higher aspirations. This is important, since physical action must have a higher purpose to be significant to humanity. Yet we need both aspects before we can create. Physical energy is empty without spiritual purpose. Spiritual purpose is useless without physical action. Our higher ideals will insure that a positive focus is our intent. This means peace over war, and compassion over anger.

The Strength represents the element of fire. As we look at the card we see a woman pictured holding the mouth of a lion. Above her head is the symbol of strength and completion. It also remotely reminds us of a spiritual halo or the positive side of our nature. The flowers that adorn her head are a symbol of great beauty and the pleasurable aspects of nature. This is indeed a special card. Her robe reminds us that purity of deed is her intention. While she holds the mouth of the lion she seems to be taming his animal passions. Perhaps this speaks to the animal passions that we must all tame to move forward on the path. At the same time, she does not seem to be hurting the lion or suppressing it. She is simply taming or teaching it discipline. It requires courage for her, such a lovely and delicate person to conquer the king of beasts. She has done it, and both seem better off. She and the lion have agreed on a balance and will now unite body and spirit as they celebrate the real pleasures of life.

Throughout the tarot we have seen the unity of opposites. Here once again is a key point.

The Strength card represents Leo, the lion. It is a card of radiance. While the Chariot reflects the illumination of the Moon, the Strength displays the radiance of the Sun. It is a card of power, authority, and dominance. Dominance over our skills and inner passions to achieve power. It is through perseverance and sheer power that we maintain the will to overcome all adversity. The concept is that spirit dominates matter. This is the higher ideal. It is important to maintain an even temper, and to keep our emotions in control, if we are to achieve the best results. Anger, jealousy, and envy are matters of the heart. Strength controls matters of the heart. It regulates positive issues of the heart as well as the negative issues. Another key issue is that of false pride. It is essential to feel secure with ourselves, for the Strength card can foretell of false pride and arrogance. Illusions of grandeur and false representation are often depicted if you have this card in your spread. Yes, it is true, the beauty of our inner hearts can have great power. It can soothe the savage beast. While we move forward to confront our obstacles straight on, we must always stay aware of our inner spirits. This is the true source of our power. It is the reserve energy we can tap into when the going gets rough. As we let go of the past we become free to express the true potential of our love and affection. The Strength card can represent people born July 21-August 21. Or it can demonstrate activities in that month.

Positive Meaning—Courage, strength, fortitude. Acting, drama, theater. Great beauty, Inner passions. Will, and desire. Authority. Victory ahead. Charisma, and radiance. Blend inner forces physical energy for success. Overcome fears tied to the past. The center of attention. Pride and self worth are needed. Move straight ahead. Get right to the heart of the issue. Get to the point. Be more observant and take your time to develop a better plan before moving. Nobility. The project is in divine order. You can insure its success through will-power and determination. A celebration is in order. Change hair styles, or visit a beauty salon. Purchase a new item at this time. A loved one is involved in the issue. Demonstrate your true feelings. Confront your opponents with wisdom and courage. Start an exercise program at this time. Stay calm in negative situations.

Detriment—You are fearful of something related to your past. You are holding on to the past. You must develop a better plan. Think it through, and look for the real meaning. Someone is deceiving you. The primal, animal passions are in control. Seek a balance, by reaching for the higher values. Someone is abusing their body. The body is ruling the mind. Weakness, ill-will, or argumentiveness. Melancholy or depression may result. False pride or arrogance should be avoided. Be more observant. Believe in yourself. Anger, jealousy, or envy is present. Fear of the unknown. Think it over before you speak. Tame the wild beast inside. Confront your problems. Develop inner strength.

Special Features

ruler   Leo
color   gold, orange, yellow
essence   frankincense, peppermint, amber
activities   curiosity, flirtation
occupations   acting, theater, beauty business, fashion design, jewelers, politicans, soldiers, managers, financiers, painters
role in life   lead by courage and action

cautions   false pride. Pay attention to details
major issue   fortitude, strength, and courage
inner feeling   charitable, and sense of radiance
love interest   traditional relationships, loyalty
residence   hot dry climates. Luxurious surroundings, gardens
trips   to centers of attraction, luxury resorts
family   desire to provide and be head of household
health   problems with circulation and back area
finances   generous, and can be fortunate in money matters
to do   keep false pride in check, avoid depression
day of the week   Sunday
expression   I radiate in the word of God. In the essence of my being, the enjoyment of life is in the beauty of every tree, every flower, and in the heart and soul of each of us.

THE HERMIT

9

The Hermit represents introspection, meditation and the search for inner knowledge. He is a wise person who is in search of the truth. As we confront the stress and strife in life, there is a need to remove ourselves from confusing environments. This time alone will best be used to place things in their proper perspective, and recreate harmony and order in our lives.

The Hermit seeks to see things just as they are. He is concerned with what is real, with what is true. There are very few frills in the life of the Hermit. He will strip the facts to the bone and examine them exactingly. It is the philosophy of the Hermit to see things just as they really are. While his insight is not as intuitive as the High Priestess, he draws on his past experiences and encounters to produce wisdom and foresight.

It is the Hermit who continues to struggle with the past. It is also the Hermit who will help us let go of the past, once and for all. The Hermit teaches us the importance of releasing the past and making a new start. He will not make this start himself, but will certainly notify us as to the new direction we should take.

As a part of the process, the Hermit will use meditation. Meditation will be helpful in isolating our feelings and thoughts on certain issues. It is the way to create silence and clarity from an environment of confusion. As a teacher and guide the Hermit is the wise person who sits alone in the tower, analyzing and criticizing the events in life. He has an uncanny ability for organizing and creating systems. He must however be careful not to spend too much time doing this, lest he become hyper-critical and cruel in his opinions.

When the Hermit has evolved, he will recognize the importance of using his judgments wisely. Everyone is not ready for the sharpness and critiques offered by him. In fact, some people will prefer not to hear what he has to say at all. They are not ready to make a change. They are still living in the past, and not ready for the possible voyage that lies ahead. Therefore, it is best, as with all teachers, or masters, that he wait for the time when he is approached and asked to share his information. He must watch out for the tendency to force his ideas and sense of morality on others. If they are not ready for it, or are of the sensitive type, they will reject it as harsh criticism.

The Hermit simply tells it like it is. He can see the right way to do something and the wrong way to do something. He does, after all, spend most of his time looking at how things work. He seems not to be as concerned about what they are, as he is about how they work.

When you meditate on the Hermit tarot card, you will notice a bearded man holding a lantern. He appears to be standing on top of a mountain. It is from here that he looks down on the world with his keen mind. From here he will form his ideas and opinions. By the way, he has many opinions about everything and everyone. The Hermit has a white beard, possibly indicating his status as the older wise person in the group. In his cloak of grey he shows some stability and an attempt to balance reality (black) with illusion (white). Together, black and white create grey. A balance of the two. Most important is the lantern he holds in his hands. It illuminates the night of darkness. It provides the information he seeks. It is the key to the mysteries of life. As he holds the lantern, the yellow light displays pure intellect. It allows him to see things just as they really are. His environment is solemn. It is austere, and he seems at peace, although he is there in isolation. With his staff in his left hand he will be able to guide himself through the confusion and the darkness by combining his intuition with his intellect. As the number nine shows, he has completed at least three journeys or reached three levels in his life. He is in meditation before he starts out on a fourth.

The journey for the Hermit is all about gaining knowledge. People born August 24-September 24 are represented by this card. Or, this may be a period when you make a major change. The Hermit is earthly, and discriminating. He will eventually receive a message concerning the higher values of humanity. It will then be up to him to begin the process of passing this message on. Although his intellect is keen, and his wit sharp, he is more passive than the Lovers, and remains earth bound, as they travel to spread the same message. He may from time to time have a restless spirit, but will soon find peace in his solitude. The Hermit teaches us how to savor and preserve life. Old age comes naturally to him, especially since it may take him many years to complete the search for knowledge. He can be very practical and pragmatic, with a respect and regard for the conventional. Unlike the Empress, his feelings are often superficial, and lack real emotion. Perhaps this is why he can organize and systematize things without becoming attached to them. The Hermit will also teach us the value of being a patient, steady worker, completing the task at all cost. He will impart the value of honesty and trust in all relationships. Unlike the duality of the Lovers, the Hermit will choose to work on one project at a time. He will complete this task before he moves on to another. The Hermit is often thrifty and realizes that success may come very slow. He will, in all his wisdom, continue to persevere until the job is done. Prudence, patience, and meditation are the important values of the Hermit.

Positive Meaning—Time to take some space for yourself. Inner wisdom, and intellect. Prudence and contemplation. You can travel now for successful business results. Take a vacation or heal yourself. Time to let go of the past and begin plans for something new. Use your abilities of analysis to see the truth. Meditation will calm your hurts and erase your fears. Rest before you begin your next major project. Attend to all details. Organize and set goals for your life. Your goals will be reached with the proper attitude. Speak your mind if someone asks your real opinion. A project in your life is nearing fruition, do not rush or force it. Be patient. Develop social skills and communication skills. Add wisdom to your criticism. Meditate, visualize, and create for whatever you want.

Detriment—Too critical. You feel negative about everything. You are spending too much time alone. Your fears are rooted in the past. Let them go. They are unfounded. You are hypersensitive. A virgo may be the reason for your current situation. Do not start a new project until you have resolved things from the past. Improper diet is the root of current health problems, or someone close to you has this problem. You are too isolated. Someone is confused about your true intentions. Learn to be more discriminating but not overly critical. You are confusing stingy with thrifty. Loosen up and have some fun. Take more time to make decisions. Use your powers of research and organization. Listen to a wiser person or consult an expert.

Special Features

ruler	Virgo
essence	lavender, peach, bergamont, orange
activities	reflection, meditation, and creative image
role in life	to show the way through wisdom and discrimination
occupations	philosophers, bank tellers, clerks, magazine writer,

editors, movie critic, accountants, dentists, nurses, technicians, politicians, lawyers, doctors

role in life   search and correct errors, illuminate the path

cautions   do not be overly critical or too sensitive

major issue   seek different solutions until you arrive at the truth

inner feeling   need to correct what is wrong

love interest   faithful and stable relationships

residence   place for solitude and meditation. Possible village or small town

trips   travel for work and teaching assignments

family   make sure all needs are met to the letter of the law

health   potential problems with poor elimination and bad digestion. Eat fresh fruit and vegetables

finances   money and wealth is slow but very steady

to do   spend some time alone to sort out your thoughts and feelings. Add wisdom to your criticism

day of the week   Wednesday

expression   The inner solitude I seek is a source of true inspiration and divine knowledge. It is through meditation and visualization that I will see the light to share wisdom with others.

THE WHEEL OF FORTUNE

10

The Wheel of Fortune represents our destiny, both good and bad. While it speaks directly to the attraction of material wealth in our lives, it also reminds us that it can be here today and gone tomorrow. The Fortune tarot card is one of great opportunity. It reflects well-being at every level. It is mental well-being, physical health, and the acquisition of material wealth. The Fortune teaches us that we can create our own destiny. No matter what hand life may deal us at any given moment, we can take control and turn negative circumstances into positive ones. This power we have witnessed in the Empress, Emperor, and in the

WHEEL ᴏꜰ FORTUNE.

Chariot. It is now time to apply these lessons for our well-being. It is time to put our spiritual lessons into effect, full-steam ahead. In the lessons of the Fortune, a positive attitude will overcome setbacks and difficulties.

We will no longer play a game of chance. No longer will we make unwise decisions, as the Hermit has taught us better. It is now time to plan, execute and win, in everything that we attempt.

We must keep in mind that we are never alone. There are always as many more good forces working with us than there are bad forces working against us. We have already learned from the Hierophant the need to maintain faith. This faith is something we may use as we need it. While the Wheel of Fortune spins around and around, so do the days of our lives. Each new day presents a new series of circumstances. These circumstances will offer new and exciting opportunities if only we keep our senses open to recognize them. There is more than one way to achieve a goal. If at first we don't make it, we should regroup and try again.

All is flux in the universe. It is ever changing, ever moving, ever presenting new people, places and things to us. There is nothing to fear, as change is the parent of progress. As it changes, we must often change to stay in tune with its heartbeat. With the knowledge of the Hermit, we will be precise and discriminating, to remain stable when it is time, and to change when it is time.

Fortune, in the form of material possessions, may be had by all. Of course there are some ways we can help insure that fortune smiles on us.

Change is what the turn of the Wheel is about. The Wheel is attached to a support. While it turns, it does not come apart from its support. One part the base of the Wheel remains stable and fixed, while the movable part spins to select a new position. Similarly, in our lives, we can remain stable through change without standing still. Once again the tarot promotes the idea of balance and harmony. Stability through change will allow us to explore, but not take a fool's journey.

The Wheel of Fortune is filled with symbolism. In each of the corners, we can find a member of the zodiac. They are not just any members of the planetary circle, but are the fixed signs. They are the taskmasters, the workers. The members of the zodiac who are responsible for turning ideas into reality. They are the winged angel, Aquarius, who brings the divine message. Next is the Eagle, Scorpio, who provides ambition and drive to whatever we do. Following is Taurus, the bull, our persevering, practical earth sign. Lastly, there is Leo the lion, who has the courage, and heart-felt desire to accomplish deeds of valor. We notice the sphinx has surfaced on top of the card, and the sign of evil is under the wheel. How we choose to live out our destiny will be in our control. Is it the way of integrity or the way of trickery and deceit? The choice is ours. There are three circles on the wheel. One for our mental well-being, one for our physical health, and one for our spiritual growth. This will be a sure path to the gathering of material possessions.

Count the spokes and determine what the meaning is to you.

The Wheel of Fortune is manifestation. It is the completion of projects and ideals. If you have selected this card, you will be reminded of its attributes. It is a reflection of the planet Jupiter, the planet of "Great Fortune." Both Jupiter and the Wheel show us that we should keep an open mind, and stay flexible to turn our fortune around. Opportunity comes and it goes. It is up to us to notice it and move on it when it comes our way. The Wheel also expects us to find new ways to express our creativity. New ways to demonstrate our skills and abilities. There is a part of life that is clear, bright, and joyful. The Wheel is the great protector. It encourages us to go for the dreams and wishes in our inner hearts. How else can you be inspired to create? Following your true heart is a process that will not only reap you financial rewards, but will benefit your emotional and physical state. The Wheel speaks to the magnificent, jovial, masculine side of our personalities. It asks us to remain calm under adversity, stay even tempered, and to share our newly acquired wealth with those following in our footsteps.

Positive Meaning—Abundance in material pursuits. Great fortune if you follow up on new opportunities. Magnetic, robust individual. Travel to a hot, moist environment. Use more wisdom to create wealth. Share your wealth for greater return in prosperity. There is an increased chance of success at this time. There are unseen forces at work to help you achieve your goals. Be more direct in asking for what you want. Take advantage of all opportunities that come naturally to you. A jovial person can be of assistance to you. Help will come when you least expect it, maintain faith in your ability to win. Expand into new arenas at this time. A health problem will take a turn for the better if you create a healthier life style. Be true to yourself. Follow your heart in making the proper choices. You will receive co-operation from others. Remember, what goes around, comes around. Act swiftly, but wisely.

Detriment—You or someone you know is not being open about a situation. There is a need to expand the vision of the project, or the goals are too limited. This is not the time to change careers. You need inspiration and motivation. Are you following your true heart in this matter? Be more flexible, and creative. A situation will be around for only a short time. You are too focused on the short term. There are more setbacks than you expected, they can however be overcome. Someone is careless, shallow, and too dependent on the opinions of others. There is a need to have further training to get the right outcome.

Special Features

ruler	Jupiter
color	purple, indigo, red
essence	carnation, cedarwood, sage, cloves
activities	help yourself and others start new projects

occupations   bankers, athletes, judges, stock brokers, professors, lawyers, physicians, priests, social workers, church workers

role in life   influence others through joy, inspiration and expansion of the higher ideals

cautions   should heed good advice, remain stable through changing conditions

major issue   luck, fortune, and protection

inner feeling   objectivity, flexibility, and feeling of empowerment

love interest   relationships with energy and spirituality

residence   bright, clear, cheerful environment

trips   travel often to follow up on opportunities after they have presented themselves

family   prosperity surround the family

health   prevent problems to hips, legs, and blood disorders

to do   take risks, expand, and live up to your true potential

day of the week   Thursday

expression   I will continue to expand and grow in the magnificence of prosperity. The light of the world shines on me as I understand, believe, and have faith in my abilities to manifest.

JUSTICE

11

The Justice card represents balance, equilibrium, and harmony. It is closely related to the aspirations of the Empress. However, in the lessons of the Justice we will see the presence is more refined and the values more developed. This is greatly due to the benefit of lessons from the Hierophant, the Chariot, and the Strength.

The Justice card will teach us to move away from false desires and hopes. It is through knowing what is right and what is wrong that justice will prevail. Through the constant activity of balance through addition, and subtraction, harmony will be gained. Proper judgment is the key to knowing what is right and what is wrong. As the Justice card reminds us of the need to stay balanced, it also speaks to the issues of fairness and discipline. In perfection the Justice will find the equality of

yin and yang, the ability to be active or the need to rest. By reaching the Justice we have entered the higher realm of consciousness. We are beginning to manifest with the wisdom expressed by the Hermit. The Justice does not have to isolate as does the Hermit. In fact, it is perhaps the most social aspect of the paths. Along this path we will meet our partners or be introduced to situations that will lead to such introductions. It is after we have acknowledged both our good and bad points that we are prepared to assimilate them. This is what effective partnership requires. A blending of temperaments for the potential of a union. The Justice also knows how to blend all the forces she has encountered. It is an interesting card. While she looks obviously female, the overtone of the card exemplifies a masculine aura. Finally the spirit and matter have become one. The male and female energies have recognized the importance of working together in total harmony.

In balancing any factors it is best to know what is too much and what is not enough. Too much physical exercise is as unbalanced as is not enough exercise. Overeating can have detrimental affects, as can undereating. Excess is a valuable lesson from the Justice tarot card. If this card appears in your spread it is possible you have a problem saying no. In your desire to win friends and please others, you may expend valuable energy on situations that are a total waste of time. Balance and harmony are represented by the scales of justice.

The Justice card also has domain over legal matters, contracts, marriages, and business partnerships.

In the Justice card, the female energy is seated holding the scales of truth, liberty, and justice in her hand. They can also represent love, beauty, and harmony. Her crown has three sections — one for truth, one for liberty, and one for equality. Or one for love, one for beauty and one for harmony. In the center there is a blue jewel, letting us know that her intentions are peaceful and expressed sincerely. The bright red robe with yellow borders is a testimony to her active energy on the physical plane. Although she uses the element of air to make her well-balanced decisions, it is the element of fire that inspires her to action. Seated between two tall pillars, she is aware of the opposing forces. It is her task to keep them in balance. The sword of knowledge and expression is held high in her right hand. It is with this tool that she will make the choice to clear the way for a new direction, or lash out with destruction and hostility. We may assume, because it is held high, that she intends to use it to enforce higher values and ideals. Her scales, held in the left hand, symbolize her main purpose. She will accurately shift things back and forth, in and out, or up and down until they are in balance to her satisfaction.

She presents herself as poised, graceful, and content. Both hands are occupied, as she is more the giving than receiving type. Her purpose is clear, she is on a mission. She sits in judgment on all things which need order and structure.

The Justice card can represent all opposites. Yin and yang, tall and short, up or down, and good and bad. She carries with her the desire to rid humanity of ugly behavior, poverty, and environmental decay. When nature is out of balance, she too is affected. She also recognizes that everything is out of balance, If one thing is out of balance. In this respect, her purpose is university. In the physical body she represents the power of self regulation or homeostasis. In the emotional area, she represents relaxation and stress management. In the spiritual realm, Justice is indicative of religious thought and belief in the higher values of human kind.

Justice will show us the way to expedite our wants and needs. Swiftness, clarity, and action are the main ways we relate to this card.

Positive Meaning — Harmony will prevail. Balance, and equilibrium is the way. Use softness, grace, and beauty to achieve your goals. Purchase a luxury item at this time. Someone should reflect more clarity. Keep to the point. Avoid scattering your energies as you have in the past. Become more stable and enjoy your partnerships. A marriage is in the near future. Move to a location with cleaner air. Avoid being influenced by false flattery. Justice will prevail to your benefit. Understand more about the laws or rules that apply to your situation. All is fair in love and war. Do what you must to win. Time to restore harmony to your life. Get rid of situations which no longer have meaning to you. Writing, publishing, beauty fields. Music or dance. People born September 21-October 21 may be involved in the near future. Simplify your life. It is too complicated, full of things that have no benefit to you.

Detriment—Watch out for schemes, unscrupulous activities by you or someone you know. You are attracting negative people because you misuse your powers. Restore balance and harmony. Moving too fast, slow down. Spend more time in nature to heal yourself. Be decisive, stop fluctuating. Try meditation to balance your depression. Develop your feminine traits more. Things out of balance. Delays due to covert or hidden intentions. Clean out old articles and garbage, they are obstacles to the future. Something needs tuning or alignment.

Special Features

ruler   Libra
color   emerald green, yellow
essence   rose, camomile, vanilla
activities   spend time in nature, environmentalists, support artistic achievements
occupations   artists, musicians, writers, gardeners, florists, judges, military commanders, beauticians, fashion designers, decorators, receptionists
role in life   to demonstrate the influence of peace, harmony, and beauty
cautions   too easily influenced, indecisive, extremist, complicated schemes that backfire
major issues   movement, resolution of disputes, teach, learn, patience, moderation, and synergy
inner feeling   balanced judgment, and perfection

love interest   partnerships and equal participation

residence   around the beauties of nature. Natural landscapes

trips   by air, travel for business

family   seek harmony and balance between children and parents. Apply thought and action. Teach moderation and compromise.

health   problems with kidneys, acid-alkaline balance

finances   result from activities of higher ideals

to do   blend the right ingredients. Pay more attention to quality vs. quantity

day of the week   Friday

expression   I seek to add balance, harmony and truth to my life. It is through the application of these virtues that my wishes and desires will manifest themselves.

THE HANGED MAN

12

The Hanged Man is a powerful but subtle card. He represents a reversal in matters of thought, perception, and action. He teaches the way in which we can change our lives for the better. One way is to change the way we see things. As the youth of the fool leads us to folly, and a carefree existence with little or no responsibility, the Hanged Man assumes responsibility and ponders ways of giving service. He is truly touched with the light of God and has surrendered to the will of universal peace.

It is often such an ever changing world that we must expand or change our views. It is this flexibility that allows us to change with the times, adjust to new situations, and stay on top of crises in our world. Without this flexibility we would remain in one of two states. One is rigid, stressful and unbending. The other is flacid, airy, and noncommital. It is through the self assurance and personality of the Hanged Man that we will be able to connect the word of God with our deeds and actions. He ponders the solutions while he pauses to rejuvenate. Waiting in these cases is not related to procrastination but is a matter of

THE HANGED MAN.

waiting for the proper time to move. He has been forced to re-evaluate his position on a subject and has chosen to call on the higher values of his faith to help him do so. The Hanged Man does not use the critical eye of the Hermit, or the physical energy of the Chariot, nor does he use the intuition of the High Priestess. He has already integrated those qualities into his personality. He now seeks the guidance of the universal spirit. He has had training along the path to surrender his inflamed ego and to replace it with confidence and faith in his own abilities.

This powerful card may require a few looks if you are to really discover the true meaning. You will see the figure on the card appears to be a younger man. At least the person's spirit is a young spirit. He hangs upside down from a wooden post. The post is in the form of a capital "T." While he hangs from only one leg, he is none the less securely attached to his base of support. He is grounded in his own place. His vibrant red leggings reflect energy and movement, while the blue shirt top indicates his peaceful demeanor. He is suspended as if he is waiting patiently for something to come to him. With his hands crossed behind his back he has decided to keep his hands out of the project. He had made a decision to leave the issue up to the higher powers. It does take a great deal of courage to wait patiently for things to form on their own. It also takes inner faith and confidence to wait suspended. On his head there is a glowing yellow light. By turning his life completely around he has received the information necessary to add inspiration and enthusiasm to the new direction he will soon be taking.

The Hanged Man is capable of accomplishing great deeds. He can overcome personality conflicts and self-centered actions that have created obstacles in the past.

Transformation is an important result of our involvement with the Hanged Man. It is he who will teach us the importance of releasing ego and dependence on the lower passions. He has the ability to transform the mundane into the magnificent. He can remove limitations and move to great heights. He is powerful, but subtle. It seems like he is just hanging around, when in reality he is allowing the hand of God to provide the direction. The Hanged Man can be comfortable with this. Especially since he has the benefit of the ten Major Arcana before him. If he has studied his lessons well, he will be in store for great things to come.

He has surrendered to the power of universal love. He is no longer afraid to show his emotions. He uses his understanding of the natural forces to emanate vitality and sunshine. In fact, many have called him a source as vital as the sun. Since he has conquered material temptations, he is no longer controlled by the world. He is now in control of the world. He has tamed the savage beast within and is waiting to enjoy the rewards. The Hanged Man is where the spirit and the material meet and manifest. He is happy that he has survived the journey and has reached the state of maturity. Many lessons have been learned, though there are still a few to be learned. He has become his own master, ready to control his own destiny. The Hanged Man recommends that we smile and maintain steadfast posture in the face of adversity. He assures us the conflict will soon pass. While it seems boring to just sit around and wait, he makes even this task interesting by using the time to do more inner building. He is devoted to the higher values of the universe. When he combines his values and his inner confidence he will move to a new level in his life. This gives him a new perspective and a new outlook on a problem he has been unable to solve.

Positive Meaning—A new day is coming. Change your position so you can get a new perspective on an old problem. Freedom from limiting relationships. Love yourself. Express your true feelings. Things in groups of three. Higher values are now important in your life. You can overcome the obstacles through patience and contemplation. You will experience a complete reversal in your favor. Have faith and trust in the higher forces. A brief delay, use the time wisely. Don't force an issue, let it work itself out. Fresh inspiration from a new source. Now is a good time to change your diet, or begin an exercise program. Get to the center of things. Be steadfast in your faith, while you change your belief system. Look at something a different way. You will see the true picture. You can harness, and transform your lower passions into magnificent benefits. Surrender to your ego and transform your bad habits.

Detriment—Someone is being self centered. Arrogance is causing a waste of time. You are seeing an important issue from only one side. Boredom is a result of not following your real heart. Someone has lost faith. The focus is too material. Need to master your emotions, and physical body. Someone feels trapped. Old habits are the cause of recent problems. There is a negative outlook involved. A fresh start is not indicated at this time. There is more work to be done.

Special Features

ruler   water
color   clear, aqua blue
essence   rose, lavender, cherry, peach
activities   contemplation, transformation, and flexibility
occupations   aquarium workers, seamen, poets, counselors, hospital workers, massage therapists, music and film producers
role in life   transform darkness into light
cautions   too sensitive, fearful, and apprehensive with self doubt
major issue   overcome personality for the transformation of negative events into great success
inner feeling   the world is one place with everybody playing a part.
love interest   deep emotional attachments
residence   near water, fresh air and warm climate
trips   to churches, sunny climates, and places of inspiration
family   creates the realization that there are higher values to be concerned about
health   problems in the circulatory system. Need to drink fresh clean water more often

finances   will come as a result of service and tranquil environments where creative projects will flourish

to do   find a suitable base from which to ground and then flow with the changes in life

day of the week   entire week

expression   I can transform darkness into light. It is the will of the higher powers that this light shine on all of humanity as it shines inside of me.

DEATH

13

The Death card represents change and transformation. When this card is selected by someone who is unfamiliar with the meaning it appears to be frightening at first. As we look into the real meaning it will soon be understood that it is anything but detrimental. In fact it is the card of rebirth and rejuvenation. The Death card represents our ability to rebound from hardships and overcome all obstacles. The aspect of death is important to any situation where a new venture is the goal. Since it is not possible for two situations to occupy the same space at the same time, one must die before the other can live. In the death of the negative, out-dated elements, the seed for the birth of positive, current elements is being germinated. Lower emotions, stagnant levels of conscious behavior will be replaced by the penetration of constructive subconscious behavior. The old dies, and it is replaced by the new. The future once again becomes bright and hopeful.

Through the lessons of the Death card, we learn the value of letting go. On the journey to the higher path, many of our wants and desires become clouded by the weariness we face in seeking their conquest. The Death card will be of great help in pointing out the self-centered aims that work to distract and hold us back from higher values. As we learn lessons in the pursuit of happiness, the toll on our physical, mental, and spiritual body is tremendous. It is through the physical body that the Death card will provide the vehicle for total rejuvenation. It is a card of intensity and will. The will to remove, destroy, and move to higher ground.

As we first meet the Death card, we have moved from the stage of the Hanged Man. We have contemplated the new direction, and are now waiting for the force of change from above. Down comes the winged eagle represented by Scorpio (ruler of the Death card) to show us the way. The way in this case is perseverance, ambition, and endless pursuit. The youth of the Hanged Man will soon be transformed into a mature conscious soul. He will live in the here and now. He will concern himself with the issues of the moment and blend his future goals with the issuance of inspiration, and constant renewal.

The skeleton on the Death card is wearing armor. There is no doubt he has decided to seek protection from what he perceives as the enemies and obstacles that stand in his way. At the same time he carries a flag representing his connection with the values of the Hierophant. His environment is surrounded with a rising sun symbolizing the birth of a new day. It also symbolizes the waters of deep consciousness that are represented by the large amount of blue water in the background. The skeleton has shown no mercy to the fallen monarch, he marches over him to eventual freedom. During any major change, something must be sacrificed. In this case the crown of the fallen king has been terminated and it is time for another ruler to replace him. Notice that the skeleton is riding a white horse. His mission is one of truth. In front of him are a religious man, a woman and a child. They will welcome the sweetness of reconstruction and higher purpose to come, after the triumph.

This is another card full of symbolism. Meditate on it and decide what other meanings you can determine.

The change made in this card is by no means a subtle one. In fact the transformation is surrounded by passion, intensity, and resourcefulness. If you have selected this card in your spread you will, realize a radial change in the near future, if it is not already happening. Your view on life will perhaps move from the personal to the cosmic consciousness. A larger and more universal outlook on the world is on the horizon. Rather than focus on the concept of death, we can look at this card as rebirth. It is the new fertile land that returns after a harsh forest fire. It is the new crop that returns after the harvest. It is the smell of freshness after the rain.

Life and rebirth are the values to focus on through the selection of this card. Keep in mind, physical, mental, or spiritual bodies are all in constant need of rejuvenation. Like the way a snake sheds the total skin, the Death card works with the Hanged Man to create a totally new reality. Often the need for total destruction becomes a puzzle to us. We will ask, "Why did this happen to me?" Not all things that appear to be negative on the outside are really negative in the long run. The process of tearing down can be a painful one. We must tear down in order to rebuild. This can refer to a relationship, career goal or even a mental attitude. A change of consciousness for the better may be just what the doctor ordered to put an important relationship back on track.

Positive Meaning — Change and transformation. Take precautions during periods of change. Let go of the old to make room for the new. Rebirth, and renewal of a situation. Use concentration to understand the obstacles. People born October 21-November 21 may be influencing this situation, or may do so in the future. Take a more radical view of consciousness. A change is imminent, no matter what you say or do. Organize and master your skills for a career change. Face the facts, no matter how difficult this seems. Electric, magnetic. You can be more powerful in a new situation. Do not fear change. *An old mind set will be replaced by higher values and a new outlook.* You may have to take something apart and then put it back together again with new parts. A baby will be born.

Detriment—Fear of change. Impulsiveness. Someone is hiding a secret. Passion has turned to jealousy, envy and revenge. Sexual misconduct. Excessive use of power. Cruelty, abusive behavior. Poor organization. Stagnation, unclear issues. Need fresh supply of ideas or concepts. Old outdated ideas. Dishonesty, self centeredness. Closed to new ideas.

Special Features

ruler   Scorpio

color   dark red, iridescent colors, maroon

essence   heather, lotus, rosemary, cypress

activities   constant rejuvenation of mind, body and spirit. Changing the old ways bringing in the new ways

occupations   surgeons, natural healers, psychics, organizers of any type, dentists, private detectives, gynecologists, sex therapists, tax consultants, government officials, butchers, secret service agents, decorators, hypnotherapists

role in life   to organize and create new forms to be used at the present time. To cut through old matter making room for the arrival of something new

cautions   too ambitious and self centered. Sexual misconduct and misuse of magnetic powers

major issue   change, transformation, renewal

inner feeling   power, intensity, and electric

love interest   physical and spiritual attractions

residence   near water, and low flat land areas. May be time to relocate to a new environment

trips   travel to new environments. Travel for pleasure rather than business

family   can overcome any difficulties in the family. Will hold the family together at all costs

finances   better with other people's money. Can gather great fortunes as a result of tenacity and hard work

to do   move on from things that have no value. Start anew
day of the week   Tuesday
expression   I am endowed with the power of electric energy. This energy may be used for the transmission of living magnetism in change, rebirth, and renewal of higher values.

TEMPERANCE

14

The Temperance tarot card represents the ability to temper, moderate, and synergize. It teaches us to blend together opposites until they become one unit. As in science, the Temperance can take even the most extreme element and adjust it until it becomes moderate. When steel is heated it melts. It transforms into another form. The Temperance exudes the vibrant energy capable of modifying, transforming and balancing.

Every living thing is vibrating, moving, and is a form of potential energy. When the need arises for two or more things to be fused together, it is the Temperance which shows us how. Through this card we learn the process of frankness, directness, and truthful communication.

From our desire to obtain the material objects in life we have been taught to play many types of games. Often these games result in hiding the truth, and deceptions. It is because of the honesty reflected in the Temperance card that we have decided to be straightforward, to speak our minds, and to face conflict head on.

The Temperance is a lesson in patience. It is through the acceptance of imagination that we are able to manifest greatness. It does however require a period of patient struggle and work to watch the transformation take place. The Temperance is similar to the Justice card. But unlike the Justice, it is more concerned with the blending together of two elements than it is with the balance of two elements. One seeks to create one element from two elements, and the other seeks to create a balanced but separate set of items. The energy of our conscious minds is a reflection of our belief system. The energy of our sub-

conscious mind is a reflection of our true feelings and purpose. Prudent, thrifty, and perceptive, the Temperance makes sure nothing is lost in the blending of the two elements. In the end, both will be better off in the new form and shape.

Temperance teaches us the value of adapting to new environments while traveling the path. It is a force of co-ordination, humility, and neutrality. Doing things to the far extreme may not be the best way to stay in control of your life. Having a system of regulation and good management of issues is a more progressive way. The Temperance is the road to the refinement of self knowledge.

The Temperance is represented by one of the major angels. The angel has strong wings which provide the basis for physical endurance, fortitude, and strength. The angel is by no means lethargic or lazy. It believes that physical energy must be used to begin the process of change. In the angel's hand are two cups. From cup to cup and back again the element will be poured, until just the right mix is achieved. The tempering of this element will give it meaning, purpose, and greater strength. The angel also has one foot in the water and one foot on land. This represents the ability of the Temperance to adapt to any environment and still project energy and vibrancy. The earth represents the practical conscious present, while the water represents the subconscious future. At some point and time the present catches up and then fuses into the future. It is a connection of time, space, and energy. On the angel's head is the halo of energy, a heavenly source of energy from a divine inspiration. The halo has empowered the Temperance with the ability to see and think clearly. In fact, as it rules our vision, it rarely misses its intended target. The mental energy allows it to carefully take aim before it attempts to hit a target. As in the Death card the sun is on the horizon alerting us to the beginning of a new day. It is located between two mountain peaks. All the symbols in this card represent the blending together of opposite elements. It is the mixing, blending, and shaping of energy until it is practical and functional to meet our needs.

The Temperance represents hot and cold, day and night, right and left, and right and wrong. It is the dawn of day and the dusk of the night. The Temperance suggests that you curb impulsive tendencies, and apply wisdom to your direct communication. While it serves to integrate polarities, it also allows combinations of things to find a common ground, or to reach a happy medium. The Temperance is inspirational, fiery, and flexible. It is one of the beautiful Major Arcana, filled with light and energy. For turning negative situations into positive ones, you may call on the energy of the Temperance. The Temperance is the card of the rainbow. It expresses the place where all the colors come together to become one grand vision. Guided by divine intelligence it moves swiftly and travels with nimble feet.

It is through the directness and honesty of the Temperance that we are able to get at the bottom of an issue. The truth is the light. The Temperance is filled with light. It is straight as an arrow. Thus when we have reached the moment of decision, it is the Temperance that will create the new element in our lives, out of the past and the present.

Positive Meaning—Synergy, blending together of opposite forces to create a beautiful new energy. Two sides to the same story. Unity of conscious and subconscious behavior. Bold, direct and frank communicator. Angelic inspiration to come soon. The future of an issue. You will be guided by divine intelligence. Let go and let the divine energy guide it. Vitality in a matter. A victory will result if you continue to regulate your physical and mental energy. Change, challenge, or synergy. The creation of something new. Unity, couples become of one mind. Alchemy, adjustments. Completion of artistic works. Coming together to become one. Persons born November 23-December 23, may be involved.

Detriment—Boldness without forethought. Too direct, which hurts the feelings of others. Spirit is separated from mind and body. Fear of transformation. Combinations may not work at this time. Strength is being depleted because of scattered energies. Someone is too impressionable. There is a conflict of interest.

Special Features

ruler   Sagittarious

color   indigo, light green, violet

essence   sage, cinnamon, musk, hyssop

activities   refines, sharpens, improves

occupations   artist, musicians, miner, medicine, law, religion, technicians, politicians, nurses, advertising, athletes, lifeguards, newspaper editors, salesman, pilots

role in life   temper, create a whole entity from parts by mixing them together

cautions   overcome worry, fear, and anxiety

major issue   attract opposites to create unity

inner feeling   joy, happiness, and desire to create

love interest   responsible but impulsive

residence   hot dry climates. Homes with space to create and invite friends

trips   short trips, not long from home front

family   love of home life and pride in family

to do   be more diplomatic in communicating with others

day of the week   Thursday

expression   The empowerment of divine wisdom has entered my being. It reflects the vitality and energy which I feel in my life as wholeness and complete satisfaction.

THE DEVIL

15

The Devil is an interesting card with several meanings. It mainly represents bondage, and self-imposed limitations. If you spell Devil backward it is *lived*. This is a contrast of values, for while the Devil prohibits and limits, the purpose of living is expansion and freedom.

The Devil is a creation of our imagination. The reality however is that what we believe in our minds may soon come to pass. Especially if we believe strongly enough. We create situations where we are chained to our fears. Greed, hostility, revenge, and envy, are the types of emotions that will sustain our fears. With the introduction of negative thoughts we are setting the path for terrible nightmares. We are prejudging outcomes and manipulating the pure intentions of otherwise good intentions. The Devil does not care about good intentions. His focus is fixed on the material, the mundane and lower levels of life. He is always subject to the imposition of temptations. Like the Devil, when our actions are designed by greed the outcome will certainly work against the propagation of higher values.

There is an important reason we have encountered the Devil, just as things were moving with such progress. After we have internalized the spiritual values of the Hierophant, mastered the courage of the Strength, and realized the victories of the Chariot, we encounter the

Devil. The lessons in life are never ending. They will continue to appear as long as we are alive. With every victory, or with every defeat, there is a new lesson to be learned. Perhaps it is an old lesson restated in a different way with a new application.

At first glance, this card presents a frightening image, very much the way the death card does. Keep in mind, that each of the twenty-two steps offers growth and development for us along our journey. Each offers a helping hand to make sure the way is constantly lit, and that we do not loose our way. The devil has the horns of the goat. A stubborn, but sure footed animal of great perseverance. The goat will succeed under the most adverse conditions, long after everyone else has given up. He refuses to be stopped by any physical limitations. His eyes reflect the intensity and seriousness that is often needed to overcome adversity. The pentagram, affixed to his head, tells us that he can either use his powers for the benefit of humanity or can become a part of Satan-like activities. He has the wings of the bat, and will no doubt seek the cover of night to perform his deeds. The night hours will limit the vision of those who would confront him about his negative deeds. The Devil is a living contradiction. The right hand is raised as if to stop something from moving forward. It motions a halt, while the right hand of the other tarot cards signals the beginning of something. Attached to the necks of the man and woman is a chain. Their hands are free. If they should choose to leave, they may. At the moment they appear to be just realizing the negative power of the Devil and will momentarily begin a motion to be set free. In the Tower they will actually assert their will for this freedom. Perhaps they have misused their intentions and have become captive of their own greed, malice, or bad intentions. Whatever the reason, they have created bondage as a result of their own negative actions. Both are nude, a carry-over from the Lovers card, where they began to explore the aspects of loving relationships. Perhaps something has gone wrong. There is a lesson one or both must learn before the relationship will succeed. The colors in this card are not brilliant and happy. In fact they do not contain the inspiration of many of the other cards. It is for this reason that you must study this card, to see the hidden meanings.

If you select this card it can reflect dishonesty, bondage, and depression. It may even foretell an illness.

Persons born December 21-January 21 are born under the sign of

Capricorn. It is through our associations with them that we will learn the values of patience, hard work, and stability.

Somewhere along the path, something or someone has entered our space and presented a temptation. The Devil has presented the possibility that we may accept this temptation and forget all the knowledge learned in the previous lessons. His lesson is direct and powerful. *Either you do or you don't. The choice is up to you.* Will you go for the Devil or will you go for life? Will you allow yourself to be depressed and sad, or will you surround your life with sunshine and light? It is necessary to confront and place negative issues on the table in front of you if you are going to overcome them. If you choose not to confront them, they will overtake your better judgment and hold you captive—a slave to our own fears—limiting you, and the people around you.

The Devil is a card of administration and organization. It will show us the way to restructure our inner fears.

Positive Meaning—You have created limitations in your life. You can remove the chains through will power and hard work. Do not give up, the light will eventually shine. There are hidden obstacles you will be face with. The situation needs fortitude and endurance. It will be a long journey. Follow the rules for achievement. Be thrifty in financial situations. There is a focus on the material, it has caused greed and selfishness. Someone is being too narrow minded about a situation that requires more expansive thinking. Time to invest in something safe. Someone is being too serious and needs to lighten up. A Capricorn may be involved. Temptation, or lower human passions. Do not give in to false pleasures. A need to check health matters. The problem is self imposed.

Detriment—Restrictions will soon be lifted. Plan carefully before you move ahead. Not the time to invest. Be more serious about an issue, but do not take it to heart. The project needs more tenacity. Do not fear the change, it will work out for the best. Stay on course, do not be led astray. Go back in time to find the root of the problem. Enjoy life more. Look on the bright side of things to find happiness. A relationship needs more attention. Replace envy, jealousy, and selfishness with more loving thoughts and deeds.

Special Features

ruler	Capricorn
color	gray, black, deep blue
essence	magnolia, bergamont, cypress, patchouli
activities	business affairs, administration

occupations   management, company presidents, bricklayers, carpenters, diplomats, negotiators, architects, farmers, miners, government workers, chiropractors

role in life   confront fears and apply will and perseverance to overcome them

cautions   selfishness and greed

major issue   proper use of power and skills

inner feeling   things will be accomplished one step at a time

love interest   stable and dependable relationships

residence   near hills or mountains. Stable environments, with office in the home

trips   long journeys, as a representative or in a diplomatic role to foreign places

family   traditional values in the home

finances   can acquire great fortunes through safe and wise investments

to do   expand thinking process, avoid tunnel vision

day of the week   Saturday

expression   In my path of happiness many stones will be unturned. Each will provide a valuable lesson which I will confront in order to see the brighter side. My task will be made easier as I lighten my burdens.

THE TOWER

16

The Tower is a natural follow up to the previous card, the Devil. In the Devil we have been asked to examine the obstacles and become free of them. The Tower represents the move to break free. Through the

THE TOWER.

Tower we learn that breaking away is not always peaceful and can often be unexpected. When something is built on false ideals or shaky ground, it will eventually fall of its own will. Similar to a house built on a faulty foundation, the slightest natural turbulence will rock its very foundation. So it is with our thoughts and actions. The idea in building something is to make it last for a long time. With just a little more energy we can begin to create elements in our life that have more quality than quantity. Things that last for long periods of time. The answer to finding more time and space for you, in such a busy life, is to build your foundations properly from the very beginning.

The Tower signifies an improper use of power, will or force. It is a demonstration of change from the highest order. As you seek to hold on to old ideals, or false realities, along comes the Tower and tears it all down. It represents quick, forceful change. In many cases this is the only thing we will learn new lessons. Misconceptions, false promises, illusions, and misrepresentation all require a new outlook if we are to ever progress. It can be in relationships, business ventures, or personal values. Being untrue to oneself is not the way. Facing the facts may not be easy, but in the long run it is the only way.

The Tower is a graphic and visual card. At first glance, it too appears to be a card of unpleasant experience. Perhaps this is true in the short run. However the Tower makes the way for the revision, and reconstruction on a more solid and valid ground. Something was established on false premises. There has been a misrepresentation, or less than admirable situation.

You will notice a bolt of lightning has struck the roof of the building. In fact it has struck with such speed and force that the top has come off. The energy and heat of the ensuing fire has spread throughout the entire structure. The lightning and fire has also caused the man and woman to flee the structure to avoid further harm. The message is clear, *this is not the way, tear it down and start over again.* Since they have knowledge of the wrong way, they will now do it the right way. It is assumed they will take their time and rebuild with caution and attention to detail. It is also hoped they will follow the dictates of their real selves, and not be affected by the misconceptions and illusions of material desire. Fortunately, in this card the people are saved from any persecution or unfair treatment. The destruction involves only that which needed to be destroyed. After realizing the truth and establishing it from falsehood, the man and woman will reconstruct life based on the higher values. This works in many areas of our lives. What often appears as a disaster actually has a hidden meaning. Sometime it is necessary to tear it all the way down in order to rebuild a better and more suitable structure.

Our higher consciousness seeks to manifest as it seeks to connect with our conscious minds. The Tower introduces the concept of the cosmic consciousness. In the previous cards, we have introduced the subconscious and the conscious minds. Here is the next level of awareness, the cosmic consciousness. A connection with the entire universe and the aspect of near total awareness.

Material ambition is a hindrance to the establishment of cosmic consciousness. This does not mean a focus on the material is undesirable. It simply means that the focus on the material must be kept in perspective. If not, a higher order will often make sure the proper balance does occur. Greed, lust, excessive ambition, and revenge will cause the tower to crumble.

You must be true to yourself. You must follow what is near and dear to your own inner feelings. Then with the proper attitude and the right purpose, rebuild and renovate the falling structure. A complete change of values, lifestyle or location is often indicated if this card appears in your spread.

True, it may also indicate an oncoming catastrophe. It will, in this case give the opportunity to make the proper adjustments. If you know something needs to be changed and you fail to do so, the outcome will be even more severe. It will only get worse instead of better.

The lesson of the Tower is two-fold. On the one hand, destruction and demolition has or will take place. On the other hand, a new set of values, or lifestyle will occur as a result. Someone will awaken to see the truth and will be forced to change as a result.

Positive Meaning—Tear down to rebuild. Energy, physical strength and adventure is needed to avoid a problem. A new business opportunity will present itself as a result of a recent loss. Re-evaluate the situation for a better solution. Unexpected and sudden changes will be for the better in the long run. Even if you do not approve or recognize it, the change is taking place at this very moment. Break free of old values. Rebuild, renovate, reconstruct, or add on to an existing situation. Eliminate all things that no longer serve your happiness and best interest. Be courageous and accept the truth. Look for a way out, there is one if you will be open to it. Break free from your lower passions. Time to get a total make-over. Purchase new furniture. A machine needs new parts. The time has come for someone to have a major change in diet. Cleanse the body of all impurities and toxins.

Detriment—Fear of change. Holding on to out-dated, impractical situations. Violence, arguments, cruelty will ensue if a change is not made. Someone is too quick to anger. Something will boil over and self destruct if the advice is not taken. Courage is needed to make a change. Weak, no physical strength. Problems will arise soon. You can find ways of resolving them. Prepare for the new day. It is here. Property, taxes, furniture and equipment may be a major issue. Ambition is blind. See the true purpose of life.

Special Features

ruler	Mars
color	red, magenta
essence	ginger, geranium, pine, basil
activities	rebuilding, restoring, awakening, healing

occupations   iron and steel workers, carpenters, barbers, solders, police, military, athletes, healers, mechanics, sales, pioneers in science and technology

role in life   tear down the old to rebuild the new

cautions   avoid anger, and the artificial

major issue   abuse of power, too much focus on the materialistic aims in life

inner feeling   freedom and competition

love interest   impulsive and headstrong in relationships

residence   rebuild or renovate

trips   unexpected journeys for business or pleasure

health   problems in the head or muscular aches and pains, sexual organs and ovaries

finances   restructure for profit

to do   make plans to prepare for the future. Get a new attitude

day of the week   Tuesday

expression   I am not afraid of the challenges presented by life. In fact I welcome changes that move me closer to my real and true desires.

THE STAR

17

The Star represents the return of hope, inspiration, and radiant energy. The Star illuminates always. While it is visible in the sky at night, it also shines on us during the day hours. It is the from the lesson of the Star that we are able to pick up the pieces and start over again. After meeting the destruction of the Tower, our very foundations have been shaken. It is necessary now to embrace a new order to the art of living. The glow of a warm spirit and the glow of hope surround us. We are not ready to embark on the acceptance of the cosmic consciousness.

How calm and peaceful life is now that we have begun to rebuild. How happy we are to finally live the true essence of our heartfelt desires. What a momentous time this is that puts us in touch with the very essence of our soul.

During the Star meditation we begin to create the inner confi-

dence we have been seeking. It will gather together our experiences and
shape them into a cosmic force. A force that will propel us forward and
upward. Visions and dreams will become reality, just as hopes and
wishes will gain the assistance of concrete actions. It is through the rec-
ognition of our true inner desires that we will be able to move forward
to their fruition. How else can we get what we want? We must face the
truth and then go after it with all our heart and soul. During the Hermit's quest for inner solitude, we learned the initial value of meditation. Now we take this personal tool and utilize its full scope.
Meditation will allow us to harmonize our physical self with our mental self. It will then permit the physical and mental to integrate with the
spiritual. Finally, as we dance in the light of the Star, these three energies will be united with the radiance of cosmic life. When this occurs,
the inner body will realize complete satisfaction. The outer body will
glow with a wonderful radiance, known as the Star!

This is a happy card, a great card to appear in your spread. A card of
good health and happy events to come. As we have learned to control
the lower passions which can lead to the destruction of our efforts, we
have also replaced them with the light of the Star. A light that softly
illuminates the pathway to love and prosperity.

Looking at the Star, the eye can feast on the beauty of all its symbolism. There is a large yellow star surrounded by seven smaller stars.
Here is the symbol of the star of wisdom shining over our heads. It
sends light to the seven smaller stars which we will later surface as
energy or vortex centers. Each will provide a source of energy in our

physical, emotional, or spiritual bodies. The lovely water bearer has chosen to look toward the water for her inspiration. With the knowledge that water is the substance of intuition and spirit, she has chosen the highest path to awareness. On the other hand she has one leg on the earth, with which she maintains contact with her material needs. Just as the Temperance has decided to connect her conscious mind with her subconscious mind. The bird of protection sits on the tree behind her. She is pouring from the cup of faith, for all to share as they arrive at the fountain of youth. Her spirit is indeed youthful and inspirational.

The Star will lead us to the understanding that we can create comfort and pleasure as we carry out even the most difficult task. The idea is to experience joy and pleasure in all things without over doing it. This is possible through inner peace. A calm attitude will allow us to stay clear regarding the path we must travel. Let your star shine. Let your love light burn bright. It will show you the way. People born January 21-February 21 will spread the word of the Star. They have the potential to show you the way.

Positive Meaning—Inspiration from above. A new concept will be successful. You will receive a merit or an award for a job well done. It is now time to act on your visions. Remain optimistic and positive. Humanity will benefit from your advanced ideas. A scientific approach is needed at this time. All of life will be elevated to a new plane as a result of a new beginning. Face an emergency head on. An idea is ahead of its time. Look inside for the faith and hope you need. Hollywood. The answer is right in front of you if you take the time to see the truth. Someone needs to be soft, gentle, but direct.

Detriment—Regain your visions and dreams. Hope and inspiration has faded. Someone has a negative attitude. You need to become clearer about an issue. A need to focus your energies. The idea is too revolutionary at this time. Ground it with a sense of practicality to make it work. Avoid friction. The cosmic influence is being ignored. Something is out of balance. Inspiration from above is being ignored. A need for inner peace.

Special Features

ruler   Aquarius
color   electric blue, sky blue
essence   orchid, camomile, lavender
activities   generosity, idealism, development of inner powers
occupations   scientific research, music, acting, aviation, nurse, technicians, nuclear scientists, inventors, electricians
role in life   connect the old and the new. Offer advice on the future of humanity. Provide hope and inspiration
cautions   keep energies focused and do not channel them in the wrong places
major issue   inspiration, mental energy, cosmic energy, meditation for self confidence
inner feeling   one step ahead at all times
love interest   mentally stimulating and romantic idealism
residence   near water and fresh air. Possible research lab in home
trips   by air, for pleasure, excitement and inspiration
family   provides bright, clear, outlook. May be sudden changes
health   problems in the ankles, legs and circulation
finances   do not be worried by financial problems. Stay focused and all will be well
to do   add practically to revolutionary ideas.
expression   I envision a shining star in the heart of every person. In me this star burns day and night, providing an inner source of inspiration and faith.

THE MOON

18

The Moon tarot card represents the inner reflection of our true selves. It stands for the clear vision of who we really are. Not who others want us to be, but who we really are deep down inside. The

Moon encourages us to believe in our dreams and visions. No matter what others may say we should be, the final decision regarding our life is up to us. One lesson of the Moon is to trust our intuition. After we have started the rebuilding process, we must believe the results will be positive. The outcome can be if we guide it in that direction. Believing in your dreams may mean you will take a few risks. That in turn means the release of fears. Especially of the unknown. Remember, what you have yet to face can not be of harm to you. The lessons of the Chariot will guide you to protection, so there is nothing to fear except fear itself. In this card there is an element of deception present. The deception is from the illusionary influence of the planet Neptune. While Neptune rules illusion, it also rules deception and falsehoods.

The Moon has a magnetic energy. It is not the same energy in the Sun or in the Star. It is a soft, gentle, flowing energy. It is a soothing compassionate, energy that seeks to understand issues through the art of being receptive. This brings us to another important point. It is therefore a need to be receptive to allow your true self to surface. How can this occur if we are not truthful with ourselves? How will others be able to help us with our wants and needs if they remain confused as to just what they are.

The Moon asks you to look into the darkness to see the light. Look where you have been afraid to look and see what is really there. Come face to face with the real truth. In this card we are still moving toward our destination. We have come a long way. We have hurdled many obstacles and learned many lessons. This is perhaps the greatest test of all. The test of self. Will it be a choice of self-deception or will it be the choice of self-realization? The choice is ours. Will we make the decision to move forward? Or will the decision be made to revert back to the old habits known before the lesson of the Tower?

We are still on the journey. The end is near. Now we must believe with heart and soul.

The Moon is shown here in several of its many faces. It is after all, the master of disguises. One phase is crescent, one is full and the other is clearly portraying the man in the moon. It too is spreading cosmic rays of gold that fall to earth. In these golden drops are the seeds of wisdom, spirit and physical well being. It is in the Moon that the human body unites with the mind and spirit. It is the formation of our complete potential. Out of the subconscious pool comes the infant crayfish. It will join the wolf and dog in their pursuit of the Moon's magnetic influence. There are the familiar two towers which let us know we have a choice to make. The blue color symbolizes the emphasis on spiritual and peaceful states of mind. It is mainly through the subconscious that the Moon is effective.

The path through the Moon may not be easiest. It can be full of obstacles. These obstacles are created by us. They are not obstacles from others, but self-induced in our own minds. Self-induced, because it is in our minds that we place the obstacles of fear, doubt, and apprehension. The Moon encourages us to listen to the inner voice. The voice inside that will illuminate the true direction. Once the truth has been recognized, the doubt will leave us forever. The path will then be clear. All our dreams and wishes will become reality. Also in the Moon is the concept of balance. The balance of practical application along with hope and belief will help get the job done.

In the lesson of the Moon the love gained from the Lovers is realized in full. It loves to love. It finds great pleasure in providing comfort and sympathy. It offers the opportunity to share its light with others who travel the path. The Moon is a reflection of higher vibrations. Its energies are subtle but powerful. It is quiet, but alert. It will teach us to reflect the image of our true self and bring that energy to fruition.

Positive Meaning—Sensitivity. Inner reflection. Belief in a positive outcome. A loving courteous person. There may be hidden fears and doubts. Speech, writing, music, theater. A Pisces person may be involved, or can help in this matter. Be more open and allow yourself to receive. Realize the truth and being deceitful. Prayer, meditation, silence may be required. A situation is nearly completed, hold on until it is. A new romance will be forthcoming. Take off your rose-colored glasses. You can change the form and shape of a relationship. Trust your intuition to lead the way. Be more practical. Let go of the old and make more space for the new.

Detriment—False hopes. Someone is being deceptive. There is a need to face the facts. Hidden enemies are creating a problem. Choose partners with more discretion. A loss of faith. This is not the time to take risks. Vacillation, laziness. Fear of the unknown. Drug or alcohol abuse. Holding to the old way of life. Taking unfair advantage. A decision must be made. Energies are scattered. Mystery and religious extreme.

Special Features

ruler   Pisces

color   violet, lavender, aqua

essence   camomile, lotus, rose, jasmine

activities   use of compassion, sympathy, and intuition

occupations   import/export, dancers, chemists, photographers, healers, sailors, seamen, shoe sales, mediums, travel agents, writers, poets, musicians, teachers

role in life   instill belief and faith where there is none

cautions   self pity—distinguish between what is real and what is illusionary

major issue   fear of unseen energies. Ability to use intuition

inner feeling   love and empathy

love interest   seeks to make relationships a romantic affair

residence   near water, in relaxing environments

trips   to new and unusual places

family   peace and harmony at all costs

health   problem areas include feet and hands

finances   success comes through the creative arts

to do   become more aware of your own inner power. Who you really are.

day of the week   Thursday

expression   I believe in all that is good. Through the power of belief and faith in myself, manifestation is simply a matter of practical application.

THE SUN

19

The Sun represents material wealth, good health, and optimism. It is the realization of our hopes, dreams and efforts. After the long journey we have at last started to see the light at the end of the tunnel. What we have asked for, prayed for and worked so hard for is now on its way to fruition. The attainment of what is ours will be achieved by maintaining a positive outlook. In the Moon we learned the importance of belief in our inner selves and our skills. Now we can apply this belief system for the manifestation of what is real and true. The Sun rules over the heart. It is the center of our energy source. Not the external force, but the internal motor of the body, mind and, spirit. The heart feels everything. It is the source of life for each of our functions.

It is through inspiration that we have created an aura of enlightenment in our lives. The choice was given to be happy or sad, and we choose happiness. We have decided to alleviate our fears through the use of our radiant energy. As the night slowly turns to day, the darkness turns to light. Soon the Sun shines bright in the sky, warming the earth and all its inhabitants. This the purpose of the Sun in our life. It will take warmth and light wherever it goes. When the body feels tired, it can be charged with the energy of nature's herbs and natural foods. When the mind is overworked, the joy of creative pleasure can be sought. When the spirit is gloomy, brighten it up with the intimacy of a loving moment. The Sun shines on us in many ways.

The Sun also brings reunions, pleasure, liberation, and motivation. It is the giver of all life.

THE SUN .

One look at the Sun tarot card and instant well-being will over take you. The Sun sits high in the sky, sending its brightest light. It also sends warmth and joy and it reflects the perfection of the moment. Each of the features is in perfect proportion, letting us know that things will balance themselves out with time. It shines down on the four sun-flowers. Each represents one of the natural elements. One flower is not fully grown, telling us that there is still some work to do in the mental, physical, spiritual, or emotional areas of our life. Perhaps in this case it is a note to attend to a physical health problem. The youth on the horse is exclaiming with joy the confidence of riding the horse with no hands. The decision has been made to let go of manipulation and authority over the horse. He has decided to use the power of his combined con-scious and subconscious energies to control the activities of the horse. This is a symbol for mastery over both the technical skills and the cre-ative skills of a project or career. When you have mastered a skill, you may then feel free to trust your intuition and approach it with a child like attitude. This will no doubt allow you to find more pleasure than tedious work effort. The garden wall has been hurdled and we are leav-ing the last of our obstacles behind.

This is a happy, joyous, energizing card. It foretells of many plea-sures to come. Victory, a happy marriage, or a good business partner-ship. There are however a few conditions. It is important that we keep the whole matter in the proper perspective. Remember the lessons of humility, and wisdom. Keep in mind the previous lessons of love and compassion. Use your power wisely. Keep your arrogance and self-centered behavior in check. Do not use your radiant energy for harmful or selfish purposes. Instead use it to nourish, energize and heal yourself and others.

In the past experiences of our journey we have witnessed the destruction of the Tower and the leadership of the Emperor. Here all the forces of good are combined. This is the physical and material manifestation of our radiance to its highest degree. All you need do is remain focused and continue to apply your previous lesson. The rest will take care of itself.

Positive Meaning—Success. Material well-being. A surprise will arrive soon. Marriage will be a success, if you trust in yourself. Energy, motivation, and wisdom are needed to complete a project. A business partnership will work if everyone cooperates equally. Teamwork is necessary. This is the beginning of something good. Lessons have been mastered. Entertainment, acting, film. Hollywood. More promotion or public relations is needed. Look beyond the surface for the real truth. It will pleasantly surprise you. Have pride in this matter. You deserve it. Someone will win something. Purchase a new ring or necklace. You are now free of something that was draining your energy. Make it so. A king or queen. Enthusiasm, regeneration.

Detriment—There is too much arrogance, and false pride involved. A matter will be delayed because of hidden obstacles. Use your own energy to get the job done. Be independent and do it yourself. Someone (perhaps you) is being too domineering and dominant. Misuse of power. A superiority complex is misleading the true purpose. Growth has stagnated. Turn up the fire. An issue needs more clarity before you proceed. You still have lessons to master. Protect yourself around other people. Someone is draining your energy. Sadness may result. Fear of loss. A new source of inspiration is needed.

Special Features

ruler	Sun
color	orange, gold, yellow
essence	frankincense, cinnamon, juniper, orange
activities	politics, leadership, inspiration

occupations   diplomats, executives, decorators, financiers, film makers, supervisors, gold smiths, actors

role in life   bring rejuvenation and energy to any situation.

cautions   monitor energy, do not allow draining situations to deplete your energy

major issue   drive, energy, light, beauty, mastery

inner feeling   self esteem, pride, warmth, superiority

love interest   kind, passionate, considerate lover

residence   in a home fit for a king or queen

trips   to centers of attraction, theme parks and capital cities

family   provides leadership and assumes role as head of household

health   problems with heart and circulation

finances   luck and success in co-operative projects

to do   balance pride and ego. Be a team player

day of the week   Sunday

expression   It is through the radiance and magnificence of my total being that I will attract success. In all that I do and say love and wisdom will guide my energies.

THE JUDGMENT

20

The Judgment is the tarot card that represents our freedom and the selection of a permanent direction. This direction will be the focus of our energy for the next twenty days, twenty weeks or twenty months. It is a card of awakening and return to action. The call from the heavens has finally reached our subconscious and we will soon be on our way to the final lesson. Since we have let it be known we are ready to return to the active life, our prayers and hard work are now reaping great benefits. We have been given the task of keeping our subconscious and conscious thoughts in balance. Through this balance, we will surrender to our true feelings. This card calls us into action. It is the revelry that sounds the beginning of the games.

Along the way, we have made the right choices. We have main-

tained a level of integrity and humility that will begin to reap great rewards.

The Judgment alerts the expectant participants to the proper time for action. Along this road you will learn that the time has now come to go all out. Now is the time! There has finally been a change of consciousness. The change has been internal and external. The entire framework of our vision is now re-structured. During this journey, many lessons have been learned. The closer we come to our real goal the more we realize happiness. In the Judgment, we are also taught to remember the lessons of the past. It is through them that we will stay focused and continue to move forward.

Once again, we have the good fortune of being exposed to a tarot card of great meaning. The angel Gabriel blows his horn to wake up the minds and spirits of two families. There are seven lines from the mouth of his horn, completing the musical scale. One representing each day of the week and the seven chakras or energy centers in the body. It is time to live life and dance to the music. Take note of the wings. In which card have you seen them? Although he emerges from the clouds, there is no storm on the way. In fact the storm has passed. He tells us the weather is fine, and all is well. The family listens with open arms. They have been waiting to arise from their coffins and re-enter life. Gabriel, who also represents fire, has always carried a message of self awareness and a call to action. He is the winged messenger who was entrusted by God with the light of the world. There is a blue sky, blue mountains, and blue waters, all indicating the use of spiritual energy. It is through the application of our new spiritual powers that we can escape the storms.

In their nakedness, all fear has been resolved. They are now ready to be fitted with a new set of clothing. Clothing that reflects the times and needs of the present day.

Responsibility and practicality lead us to have a sober mind. With a balanced and practical approach, we will actually be able to carry this message to others. It will be through our deeds and actions that they will receive this message. Judgment shows us what to do next. It instructs us in the way of sound and fair decisions. Making judgments based on preconceived ideas is not the way. People who make judgments and do not have any facts are making one-sided decisions. Likewise, those who make decisions based entirely on intuition may need more facts. It seems the best decision makers will use a combination of subconscious and conscious information. That is logic and intuition.

There is a suggestion here, that if you keep your senses open, you will see and hear the truth. As they say, the truth shall set you free. Positive energy from above has blessed the man, woman and child. They have weathered the storm. It is now time to reach the last step on the path.

Positive Meaning—Sound judgment. Social, career, and personal decisions can be made with clarity at this time. Something decided on now will last the test of time. Look at the whole picture to see the truth. Judgment requires objectivity and openness. New forms and ways of doing things will have success. Utilize all of your skills and powers. Time to go all out. Forget past hurts and go for it. A new cycle is emerging. Be broad-minded and trust yourself. Now is the time to break old habits. Be daring, courageous and results will come. Aries, Leo or Sagittarian people may have an influence on this matter. It may be time to change your location. Keep your real purpose in focus. Dance, music or entertainment. Be clearer in your communication process. Others need to hear exactly what you are saying.

Detriment—Narrow-minded thinking. Someone is being too judgmental. More courage and strength is needed. Take time to plan your trip carefully. There is negative criticism. Communications are not clear. The message is fuzzy. There is a need to be more creative. Strengthen relationships. The search continues for peace of mind.

Someone is trying to tell you something. However, you are not ready
to hear it. Eagerness and extreme attitudes may not produce positive
results.

Special Features

ruler   fire
color   red, blue, yellow
essence   cinnamon, nutmeg, bergamont, lime, rosemary
activities   movement, action, vibrations
occupations   leaders, firemen, executives, actors, athletes, parents,
fashion designers, models, healers
role in life   call others to action, inspire through pure energy
cautions   execessive physical energy may cause accidents. Think
before you leap
major issue   objective decisions. Balance and harmony in all
changes
inner feeling   warmth and energy
love interest   positive relationships based on mutual exchanges
residence   in warm climates, where the air is clean
trips   short journeys that may be unexpected
family   responsible actions that lead to growth and happiness
health   circulation, heart, head, and hips are problem areas
finances   success results from the expression of the true self and
collaboration with others
day of the week   entire week
expression   I empower through the expression of strength, courage
and action. Together, we can build a new world, a world that will be
based on peace, love and wisdom.

THE WORLD

21

The World tarot card represents the universal way of thinking, acting and being. It is the arrival at our destination. After the arrival we

THE WORLD.

are able to enjoy the fruits of victory and begin to set out on the next journey. The World reflects the bringing together of our best qualities. The qualities that remain after all lessons are complete. It is the nectar and cream of the crop. It is the celebration after the victory. Once and for all we have reached the peak of our journey. The place where others recognize the oneness of our spirits. We can now relax and have fun. The cosmic dance of life is ours to enjoy. All three levels of consciousness have come together in unity and purpose. All our inner powers, our outer desires, have joined with the universal order of nature and decided to act in unison. This is the alignment of resources for what we may call perfect harmony. The energy of the World is neither male or female. It is the operation of both energies in total harmony. They have understood the philosophy of yin and yang, of positive and negative. The lessons of the Empress and the Emperor have been internalized and all conflicts have been resolved. The power plays of dominance have been transformed into willful co-operation and mutual respect.

It is through the World that we can realize the fruits of our hard work. There were many times when we thought about turning back, giving up and facing defeat. Through the Chariot, the Strength, and the Temperance, we made the decision to continue forward. To continue on to victory. Now the payoff has placed us in the center of it all.

The dancer in the World tarot is surrounded by a wreath of life. It is tied at the top and bottom by a red cloth of action and vitality. In each corner of the card we notice the four elements. The human figure is the air sign Aquarius. This represents humanity and the human qualities in our higher values. The bird is the eagle in the Scorpio energy. It too has decided to evolve from the snake into a high flying symbol of stability and positive energy. It also represents the emotional condition of the water element. In the lower right hand corner is Leo the lion. He is our fortitude and courage in all matters of the physical world. As he represents the fire element, his energy is protective and vital. Taurus the bull completes the foursome, with his stable and practical approach to all things on the material world. As the last of the four elements, it is the manifestation of the earth element. In each hand, the dancer holds a wand or baton. They will no doubt be used to direct the global symphony that will ensue from the complete harmony of combined energies. The violet scarf wrapped around the nude body indicates the arrival at the highest point of spirituality. It is the symbol for universal consciousness. This is the final state of consciousness.

The concept of total enlightenment is one of wholism. It is where all things have come together. The image of the World as the planet Earth is a familiar one. International and national activities are regulated by this card. Certainly, the inner workings of nature are included here. It is remarkable how nature has integrated the essence of flowers, trees, animals, rain, sunshine and of course humans into one realization. Through the World, we are reminded of the importance of protecting our planet and its ecology. Living in the world means also maintaining a balance. It is the human consciousness manifested along with the subconsciousness of nature at work in harmony, lest we forget it was here before us, and in some form will be here long after we have left it.

Positive Meaning—Arrival of universal consciousness. Victory and total triumph. Affirmation and positive belief system. Moving in a new direction with success. A journey will begin soon. Joy and harmony with nature. Holistic outlook. Alignment of body, mind and spirit. International activities. Environment and ecological issues. Perfection and enlightenment. The arrival of something that will bring great joy. You will soon reach the ultimate goal through this process. World issues will be of concern to you in your new direction. Give service to humanitarian issues. There will be a great victory if you stay humble and direct your actions to a central focus.

Detriment — You are working too hard and need to find a natural source of pleasure. You are creating your own obstacles. Avoid feeling despondent. Make sure all safety precautions are taken. There is a need to become more thrifty. Be more patient and continue to persevere. Some obstacles and delays will present themselves. Hard work will help overcome them. You need to find inner peace.

Special Features

ruler   Saturn

colors   magenta, black, white

essence   cypress, magnolia, myrrh

activities   bring energy to move a situation to a conclusion

occupations   miners, travel agents, peace corps worker, research scientists, accountants, business managers, gardeners, government workers, insurance agents, chiropractors, dentists, librarians

role in life   display the rule that hard work and learning lessons will achieve great results

major issue   success and triumph after the great journey

inner feeling   power and organization

love interest   conservative and traditional values

residence   in well-established areas, or near mountains and farmland

trips   travel soon to complete a transaction

family   seeks security at all costs

health   problems with teeth, colds, and glandular system

finances   economy and frugality bring success

to do   overcome narrow outlook on life

day of the week   Saturday

expression   After testing my faith and endurance, I have overcome all obstacles. There will be a grand celebration at the end of my journey to include the cosmic dance of life.

8

MINOR ARCANA

The Suit of Swords

Ace of Swords

A hand emerges through a cloud of doubt and confusion. It carries the crown and branches of sincerity and compassion. The hand glows with an aura of white light, expressing its intent to struggle for what is right and pure.

Positive Meaning—The beginning of a new idea. Conquest or victory. A journey by air. Individuality. Creative forces will soon come together. Mental energy of great force. Determination, force and action.

Detriment—Think before you act. Violence, obstacles of an intellectual nature. Justice will be served. Confusion and doubt. More facts to gather. Need to organize ideas.

Two of Swords

The crescent moon overlooks a woman who decides to withdraw from the moment. She appears to be blindfolded and in deep concentration. Behind her a tranquil body of water where she has come to ponder life.

Positive Meaning—Balanced mental energy. Establishing a rhythm. Firmness. Temporary escape from reality. Need to balance ideas and desires. Make a choice between two of something. Togetherness.

Detriment—Indecision, possessive, escape from reality. Inner conflict. Tension in a partnership. False information.

Three of Swords

Three swords pierce a bright red heart. Three clouds and rain appear in the background.

Positive Meaning—A past hurt has lingered on. Stormy weather ahead. A separation may occur. Arguments, disagreements. Internal conflict between actions, thoughts, and desires. Evolution, negative thinking.

Detriment—Holding on to past sorrows have caused pain in the present. Negative thinking will affect all parts of your life. Possibility of mental breakdown. Possible loss.

Four of Swords

A man is resting in the solitude of the church. He ponders the sorrow and strife in his life. He seeks isolation for this purpose.

Positive Meaning—Rest and recuperation. Solitude. Religious experience. Many thoughts at one time. Healing and mending. Waiting patiently for the next idea.

Detriment—Be cautious. Proceed with caution. Search for the true meaning. A return to action. Be thrifty.

Five of Swords

A person holds the swords of the other people. He has captured them, or they have surrendered to him.

Positive Meaning—A victory. Someone has been defeated unfairly. An unexpected defeat. A victory that was won unfairly. Ambition. Embarrassment.

ACE of SWORDS.

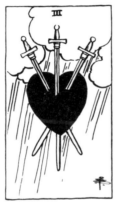

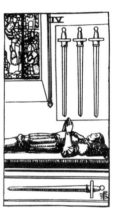

Detriment—False pride. Loss or defeat. Weakness.

Six of Swords

A man, woman and child move across the water in a boat. They are leaving the present location with the hope of finding a better situation.

Positive Meaning—Things will be better on the other side. Be objective and see the entire picture. Focus your thoughts on moving through obstacles. Success after problems. A person will deliver something for you. Journey or trip.

Detriment—The obstacles must be worked through. No movement. Things have not been resolved yet.

Seven of Swords

A brilliant yellow background surrounds a man walking with five of the seven swords in his hands. He is careful not to disturb anyone in his haste to leave.

Positive Meaning—Leaving with the ideas of others. Loss to theft. New plans or ideas. Partial success. Something requires a little more effort. Biting off more than you can chew.

Detriment—Plans may fail at this time. Someone may be attempting to take something. Arguments, uncertain facts.

Eight of Swords

A woman is now blindfolded and surrounded by eight swords.

Positive Meaning—Someone has been indecisive and has caused a situation to come to a halt. Prisoner of one's own fears. Narrow minded outlook on life. Mental fatigue. Take a break. Confusion and doubt. There are no other options at this time.

Detriment—New beginnings. Release from self doubt and fear. Objective and expansive view.

Nine of Swords

With the darkness of night in the background a troubled person has been awakened in the night. It is possible that sleep has been interrupted by worries and thoughts of a situation out of control.

Positive Meaning — Worry, broken promises and anxiety. Poor self image. Suffering. Possible illness. Burden belonging to another personl. Isolation, doubt. Make inner peace.

Detriment — Positive outlook based on patience. Time will correct the problems. Pain is slowly leaving. Rest.

Ten of Swords

The swords in this card are actually placed in the back of the person. Helpless and apparently in pain, the person simply lies on the shore awaiting help.

Positive Meaning — Unexpected loss. Self-inflicted pain. Ideas of jealousy and revenge have backfired. Defeat and fear of loss. Disappointment.

Detriment — Problems will slowly fade away. Now is the time to move ahead. Think your way out of a negative situation.

Page of Swords

A young person holds a sword with both hands. He (may also be a female) looks over his shoulder as if something is following him. He is quick and is energetic.

Positive Meaning — A message will be received which will require immediate attention. A builder or singer. A message bringer. Move swiftly but think first. Perception of the unseen before it happens.

Detriment — False pretenses. Need more preparation. Illness.

PAGE of SWORDS.

KNIGHT of SWORDS.

QUEEN of SWORDS.

KING of SWORDS.

Knight of Swords

A knight charges on a fast moving horse. He has his sword drawn and wears a serious expression.

Positive Meaning—A call to immediate action. Self defense in the face of adversity. A message is on its way. Protect virtue and integrity at all costs. Courage and action. Bravery and futuristic ideas. Bad luck is leaving. Take a journey to clear your mind before starting a new project.

Detriment—A matter is just arriving. Impulsive and spontaneous actions. Violence and anger. Slow down and get a hold of yourself. Arrogance.

Queen of Swords

The Queen of thought sits on a pedestal and looks to the future. She is quick with her wit and also has the ability to use her mental powers for great achievements. She is known as a perfectionist and uses her sword to sharpen her quick wit.

Positve Meaning—An intelligent woman who has great mental powers. She is sharp, and witty. Her character is strong although she has known the meaning of pain in her life. Divorce yourself of prejudice and subjective feelings. See the entire picture before you decide. Clarity and fairness, even after pain and hurt.

Detriment—Narrow minded thinking. A woman who will bring pain and suffering. Mourning and loneliness.

King of Swords

The King sits on the throne, concerned with the present. He is a fair and just ruler. It is his decision to weigh all matters that are presented before him. He is quick and intelligent.

Positive Meaning—Lawyer, counselor or media expert. He is clear and focused. Action and determination. Experience. Justice. thoughts and ideals of high human value. Military or authority. Wisdom, good advice. Possible legal situations.

Detriment—Unfair biased decisions. A cruel and dangerous person. Lawsuits and legal entanglements. Prejudice. Lack of clarity. Conflict. Disruption. Suspicion.

CUPS

Ace of Cups

A card of much happiness. The cup is held gently in a hand that extends from a clouded area. The dove of love and harmony places the forces of nature into the cup. Five streams of water pour from the cup into the sea of emotions. As our five senses open and become aware, each stream guides it to the proper place. From the cup we can drink the nectar of life.

Positive Meaning—The beginning of a love affair or great romance. Beauty and love of life and nature. Spiritual awareness. The inner beauty of your spirit. Fun, pleasure, and happiness. An emotional situation. Fertility and good blessings. Growth and regeneration.

Detriment—Need for more love and wisdom Affairs of the heart must be approached with caution. A need for spiritual activities. Delays in matters of the heart.

Two of Cups

A man and woman hold two cups. They both wear wreaths. His is one of action and courage. Hers is one of health and prosperity. They are faced with a decision. Since the cups are in hand, the potential of happiness is there should they choose to move in the proper direction.

Positive Meaning—A deep and sincere love affair. A partnership of great rewards. Sincerity and health in all matters. Balance. Sharing, co-operation. Mutual respect.

Detriment—Sadness and a broken heart. Two people can not get together because of obstacles. Temptation has interrupted a relationship. Separation.

Three of Cups

Three female figures hold their cups up in celebration. They are surrounded by fruit and flowers. Each has a look of contentment.

Positive Meaning—Contentment and happiness. Fulfillment and completion. Compromise. Fertility and abundance. Pleasure. Joy at a spiritual level. True happiness.

Detriment—Excessive pleasures. Over-extension of the heart and soul. Too focused on the physical aspects. Need for spiritual enlightenment. Need for sexual discipline.

Four of Cups

Apparently in rejection a man sits under a tree with his legs crossed. He meditates on the three cups in front of him. Another cup is being offered from the clouds. It may or may not be what he is expecting.

Positive Meaning—A romance is presented, but not the one that fulfills the desires. Meditation on the true meaning of life. Questions concerning the need for love and spirituality. Need for inner peace and happiness.

Detriment—Something new is on the horizon. Wait patiently. A new relationship will bring fulfillment. Renewal and rejuvenation. Time to start again.

Five of Cups

A man in a long black cloak stands before five cups. Three of the cups

ACE of CUPS.

are turned over and two are still standing. He is in front of a stream that separates him and a building. There is a bridge in the background that leads to the land on the other side. Notice the color of the liquid from each cup.

Positive Meaning—Regret. Displeasure. Sorrow. A separation has caused sorrow. There is still enough left to rebuild. Imperfection. Emotional let down.

Detriment—Return of joy. Hope. Reunion.

Six of Cups

A young boy and a girl stand in a yard. He offers her a cup with a white flower. She looks at him with joy and appreciation. They are surrounded by five other cups.

Positive Meaning—Things to do with past memories and childhood. Friends from the past may re-enter your life. Share your friendship with another. Joy and pleasure is coming soon.

Detriment—Forget the past and move on. Memories of the past are of concern. Live for the future.

Seven of Cups

A man looks at seven cups. Each is filled with a different image. The choices range from the snake of animal passion to the wreath of love and victory. Take a good look at each cup. He is tempted to take the wrong cup. Which one is the right one for him? He must separate reality from illusion.

Positive Meaning—Fantasy. Illusion, false hopes. Many decisions. Useless day dreaming.

Detriment—Focused attention on an issue. Be clear on your choices. Take the higher path. Determination and direct energy.

Eight of Cups

Clearly, a man has decided to leave his present conditions. He moves up the hill to another location. The eight cups remain as they were, stacked on one another.

Positive Meaning—Abandonment. Tired. Need for a mental and spiritual break from stress and strain. A choice to move to something with more meaning. Journey away from emotional ties. Fear of romantic involvement.

Detriment—Return to happiness. Hold on to what you have for the time being.

Nine of Cups

A man sits with his arms folded in satisfaction and contentment. As soon as you see this card, make a wish. The cups in the background are neatly stacked and are waiting to be filled with his pleasures.

Positive Meaning—Material pleasure can be had by all. Add joy to everything you do. Celebration of a major emotional triumph. Everything in your life should please you. Material and emotional well-being. Happiness.

Detriment—Some happiness, but not all the time. Opposition. Obstacles. Emotions are not sincere.

Ten of Cups

A man, woman and two children stand in front of a country home. The children play happily while the man and woman enjoy the environment and the moment of pleasure.

Positive Meaning—Family happiness. The purchase of a new home. A happy marriage. Honor. Virtue, Emotional satisfaction. All things good.

Detriment—Unhappy family life. Problems with a child. Conflicting ideas and emotions.

Page of Cups

A young man looks into a cup. The cup contains a fish which looks back at him. He stands in front of a flowing stream, and wears a smile on his face.

Positive Meaning—Reflection of the inner self. Self-awareness. Channeling, and spiritual divination. Studies, or need for spiritual information. Love of self. Loyal, friendly person of great sensitivity.

Detriment—Deception, untrustworthy, shy person. Hidden truths. Take a good look at yourself. Be clear about all intentions.

Knight of Cups

This person is dressed in armor. The armor is protecting his emotions. At the same time he carries a cup with confidence and ease.

Positive Meaning—Graceful, poetic style. A message will be received soon. It may be an invitation to a social event. Spiritual message. Love and romance are on the way. Proceed with style. Take your time.

Detriment—Be cautious about messages. Living in a dream world. Need to put feelings into action. Examine everything closer.

Queen of Cups

The Queen is a beautiful, feminine woman. She knows her powers and is secure with her inner being. She teaches the value of love and compassion. In her hand she holds her cup of wisdom. She glances into it for any answers she may need. Her world is spiritual and intuitive.

Positive Meaning—Loving, devoted person. Can turn dreams into

PAGE of CUPS.

KNIGHT of CUPS.

QUEEN of CUPS.

KING of CUPS.

reality. Has an open heart. Good wife and mother. Creative arts and the feeling of enjoyment that accompany them. Pleasure and beauty, style and grace.

Detriment—Be cautious with a new person in your life. Emotional discord. Sensuality over compassion.

King of Cups

The King sits in his chair and looks to the immediate future. He holds two objects in his hands. The water that surrounds him is experiencing movement and the influence of other forces.

Positive Meaning—A reliable man. Of deep commitment. Knows the law and is adept in matters of the business world. He is a good leader, husband and father. Creativity. Religion. Artist. Scientific research. Responsibility. A good counselor.

Detriment—Unreliable person, doubt, loss of faith. Dishonesty. Emotional turmoil. Need to regain spirituality and intuition.

WANDS

Ace of Wands

The hand of enterprise and action comes from a cloud. The wand has leaves of prosperity. It is held by a hand surrounded in white light.

Positive Meaning—This is the beginning of a business or financial undertaking. The birth of an idea. Action and courage in a matter of business. Physical well being and good health. Fertility and a happy life ahead. Creative energy and new inventions. A new adventure.

Detriment—Now is not the best time to launch a new idea. Something may be postponed. The inner desires are being ignored.

Two of Wands

The person stands at the head of the situation and looks at the globe in his hand. He has decided to stand in between two wands. Both have the potential for growth. He does however pay attention to the one that is not anchored to the balcony.

Positive Meaning—Success in business and growth. A decision has been made. Partnership and togetherness. Reality. Integration of two or more forces. An influential person. Employment, motivation and executive leadership.

Detriment—Boredom. Not a good time to form partnerships. Physical pain. Wrong decision has been made. Use more intuition.

Three of Wands

With the benefit of a brilliant yellow background, the man now watches his ships come in. He is surrounded by three wands. He is no longer placing his focus in front of him, but looks far off into the distance.

Positive Meaning—Realization of dreams and desires. Established business person. Be practical. Wealth and power. Physical strength. Honesty and integrity. Trade and business deals. Money will start to come in from past situations.

Detriment—Be aware of false pride and arrogance. Listen to others, but be aware of deception. Peer pressure. Guard profits.

Four of Wands

Flowers and an aura of celebration display the festive atmosphere of this card. There is a wreath of flowers connecting the four forces of nature. Everything is in harmony.

Positive Meaning—Harmony, celebration after the victory. The celebration of a romance. A partnership or wedding. Harvest of benefits. Satisfaction. Positive feelings for everyone.

ACE of WANDS.

II

III

IV

V

VI

VII

Detriment—The same as above. Matters could have been better, but the present results are acceptable. There may be some insecurity.

Five of Wands

A group of five young men wield their wands amidst a blue sky. The ground is barren and the terrain somewhat rough. It appears they are in conflict with one another. Apparently they are wasting energy on a negative pursuit.

Positive Meaning—Inner conflict. Opposition. Frustration. Anxiety. Plan your strategy carefully. Courage is needed. Work and production. Some obstacles. Stay centered and focused.

Detriment—Generosity. Free of conflict soon. Victory can be had through courage. Train for an upcoming event.

Six of Wands

The subject rides a white horse that is wearing a green overgarment. The horse appears proud and stable. The rider holds a wand in the air. It has a wreath of victory attached. Also he wears one on his head as his associates march at his side.

Positive Meaning—Celebration after a great victory. Help is on the way. A time to regroup and re-apply yourself. Belief in yourself. Nobility and pride. Inspiration. Good news is on the way.

Detriment—More physical and mental energy is needed for victory. Fear. A delay is temporary. Believe in your abilities to succeed.

Seven of Wands

A young man stands firm against the six oncoming wands. He seems to be seriously involved in protecting his position. The blue sky in the background alerts us to the struggle for inner peace.

Positive Meaning—Stand firm under adversity. Victory through courage. Inner fortitude and courage. A challenge is present. Issues will be resolved soon. Advantage. Honor.

Detriment—Doubt, fear, and anxiety.

Eight of Wands

Eight wands are in flight through the air. Depending on your view, they are just leaving or are coming to rest. Each has three sets of leaves. Mind, body, and spirit are aligned.

Positive Meaning—A journey is beginning or about to end. Swift and quick movement. Direct action. Moving fast. Goals are in sight. Speed. Send a message to someone.

Detriment—Jealousy. Things are moving too fast. Slow down. Anxiety. Delays. Ground yourself.

Nine of Wands

An injured subject stands in front of eight wands. He holds the ninth in his hand. Notice the expression on his face as he watches over the wands.

Positive meaning—A health issue. Overcome all obstacles. Keep a watchful eye. A business or career issue needs careful planning. Hidden obstacles.

Detriment—Obstacles. Avoid physical injury. Some delays, a rest is needed for rejuvenation.

Ten of Wands

A man with yellow hair carries ten wands toward a city or town. Perhaps he has organized the many ideas and has found a solution to a difficult problem.

Positive Meaning—Burden. Too heavy a load. Organize your scat-

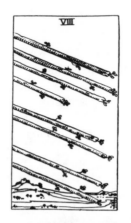

PAGE of WANDS.

KNIGHT of WANDS.

QUEEN of WANDS.

KING of WANDS

tered ideas. Present a proposal. Limitations can be overcome. Depression caused by too much work. Remove excess baggage from your life.

Detriment—Too much to handle at this time. Feeling guilt, anger, fear or jealousy. Hard work ahead.

Page of Wands

A younger person, male or female, stands in expectation, holding the single wand firmly. The posture is anticipatory but confident. The call to action will soon be sent or received.

Positive Meaning—Favorable news will come. Send a message by a younger person. Beauty. The green light is on. You may proceed. A small victory will lead to larger ones. Be patient. Individual development. A lover.

Detriment—Instability. News may not be what you wanted to hear. Not the best time to move. Protect yourself in matters of the heart.

Knight of Wands

A representative moves into swift action. He rides a horse that will move at the necessary pace. Energy action and courage travel with him. Dressed in armor, he is ready to protect his material and spiritual assets.

Positive Meaning—A situation will change quickly. Some force and strength may be necessary. A trip will require extra energy. Plan ahead to avoid mistakes. A change in living conditions. Money will be coming soon. Growth and inspiration.

Detriment—Develop a new approach to an old problem. Protect yourself from hidden foes. Start an exercise program now. Delays and obstacles to your plans.

Queen of Wands

The Queen looks away from the present conditions. She holds a wand in one hand, and a sunflower in the other. Many symbols surround her throne.

Positive Meaning—A powerful woman. Good in business and financial matters. Perhaps a Leo, Sagittarian or Aries. She has practical knowledge and knows how to apply it. She also has endurance and great energy. Friendly and honorable. Passionate and loving. Positive energy. Love of home environment.

Detriment—Prejudice, jealousy. Energy out of control. Wasted efforts. Fearful and hard headed. Burnout, stress. Too much control.

King of Wands

The King faces the past. He also holds a single wand in his hand. His flowing robe tells us he is expansive and open minded. Possibly a Leo, Sagittarian, or Aries male.

Positive Meaning—Authoritative, honest person. Helpful and sincere. A friendly, intelligent male with courage and strength. Action and noble application. Handsome and considerate. Accepts new opportunities with open arms. Not afraid of new situations. Leadership potential.

Detriment—Move without careful plans. Too impulsive. Haste makes waste. Domineering control over others. Too much. Excessive.

PENTACLES

Ace of Pentacles

As in the other aces, a hand shows itself through a cloud formation. This time it holds a single pentacle. In the area below is a gateway to the mountain peak.

Positive Meaning—Beginning of prosperity. Money and the attainment of good things in your life. Situation will present itself for career advancement or a business development. Happiness and material gain. Houses, furniture, cars, clothes, presents, gifts. Employment. Physical and material combinations.

Detriment—Wealth, but not with inner peace. Greed. Bad decision concerning the use of material resources. Not the best time to begin a new financial plan.

Two of Pentacles

The man shifts his weight back and forth as he attempts to balance the two coins. Ships in the sea of the subconscious move in the waters behind him.

Positive Meaning—Balance work and play. Balance an account. A decision between two elements must be made. You may be able to have both. Prosperity will result if you maintain inner harmony and spirituality. A change in material or financial status will occur soon. Stay focused.

Detriment—Make a decision. Only one element can work at a time. A message is forthcoming. Stay flexible, you are too rigid.

Three of Pentacles

A craftsman works in front of two onlookers. He also explains his work as they ponder the progress.

Positive Meaning—Skill, technical ability. Knowledge of a profession is nearing the master level. Clarity and perfection in your work or ability to generate finance. Start the process, help will come when you need it.

Detriment—Still work to be done. Criticism of your skills. Stay grounded and produce work that has meaning. Seek a second opinion. Take a class or workshop.

ACE OF PENTACLES

II

III

IV

VI

VII

Four of Pentacles

While he sits, this person remains in tight possession of four pentacles. One on his head, one in his arms and two at his feet. His red undergarment shows his intent for action. However, he holds on with some sign of uncertainly.

Positive Meaning—Ability to provide material needs. Hold on to stability. Power. Success, Material gain. Material prosperity above spiritual enlightenment.

Detriment—Holding on too tight. Let go. Inability to share. Insecure about skills and abilities.

Five of Pentacles

A man and a woman are in a snow storm. He is injured and she appears to be cold. There is however, a light of hope coming from the stained glass window. The five pentacles are placed in this window.

Positive Meaning—A loss of finance. Impractical decision. Some obstacles, but stay hopeful. Possible physical illness. Help is needed. Distress and material troubles.

Detriment—Hope and faith will turn a bad situation around. Good news on the way. A new situation is developing. Spiritual influences are on your side.

Six of Pentacles

A businessman holds a scale in one hand and passes out coins with the other hand. There are two people who seek his assistance.

Positive Meaning—Accomplishment and completion. Help to the needy. A wise business investment. Kindness. A gift will be given or received. Share and care about others. Use wise judgment in your financial and material pursuits.

Detriment—Unwise investments. Poor choice of friends and associates. Plan everything carefully before you do it.

Seven of Pentacles

The worker stands and examines the fruits of his labor. He is attempting to make a decision about something. In his hand is the tool of his trade. Behind him is a violet field where his work will hopefully lead him.

Positive Meaning—Hard work and perseverance will result in success. Stop for a moment and look over your progress. Money is on its way. Make sure you get what it is worth. Do not shortchange your efforts. Your material efforts are being questioned because of a loss of faith.

Detriment—Faith and hope are in question. Slow down. The obstacles are temporary. If growth continues, you continue. If growth does not continue stop and find another method.

Eight of Pentacles

In this card, the worker or technician is increasing the production of his items. He works away from the center of activity and seems to be involved with his project.

Positive Meaning—Employment will arrive soon. Study may enhance your skills. Stay focused and apply your practical skill for success. Take your time and pay attention to important details.

Detriment—Work efforts are rushed and not your best. Employment may be difficult at this time. You are focusing on quantity and not quality.

Nine of Pentacles

In a beautiful country garden, a person holds a bird on the left arm. The right hand rests on one of the nine pentacles. There are six on the right side and three on the left side. This card is filled with symbolism. What else do you notice?

Positive Meaning—Individual happiness and prosperity. Personal goals are achieved. Love and enjoyment of natural elements. Mental, physical, and spiritual actions are in complete alignment. Rely on your own abilities.

Detriment—Protect yourself. Seek help if needed. Have more faith in your own abilities. A new personal direction may be necessary. Spend more time in nature or take a break from work efforts.

Ten of Pentacles

A family occupies the space where they live or work. The pentacles surround them in great abundance.

Positive Meaning—Group efforts will be successful. Co-operation is essential in gaining material gain. The wisdom of elders and experienced professionals will help. An inheritance is forth coming. The home is secure and happy. Property or family issue are at hand.

Detriment—Play it safe at this time. Use the wisdom and experience of others to help your decision. A family member may need your help.

Page of Pentacles

A proud young man holds a single pentacle high in the air. He looks it over and moves toward the future.

Positive Meaning—Possibly a student or a person about to study something. Through understanding of how something works, we can better utilize it. Good news. New and practical ideas. Enthusiasm.

Detriment—More research is needed. Be more practical and enthusiastic. Stay grounded.

PAGE of PENTACLES.

KNIGHT of PENTACLES.

QUEEN of PENTACLES.

KING of PENTACLES.

Knight of Pentacles

An armored messenger comes to a halt. He carries a single pentacle. In the background is a brilliant yellow. A red stream flows beside him.

Positive Meaning—Patience and inner confidence. Energy that is disciplined. Messenger with news of money. Stability and practical actions. Responsibility. Do not bite off more than you can chew.

Detriment—Be more active and flexible. Think of making a location or employment change. Tunnel vision. Stagnation and instability. Worry and obstacles.

Queen of Pentacles

Perhaps one of the most beautiful of all the Minor Arcana. The Queen sits on her throne. She is surrounded by all the wonders of nature. There is clarity in the yellow air. Spirituality in the blue stream. She has energy and courage in her red robe. At the same time roses and green plants symbolize her stability and wealth.

Positive Meaning—Wealth and well-being. A woman of practicality and reliability. A good business woman who is also blessed with good common sense. She is a woman of great wealth. A nature lover. Security. Satisfaction with results.

Detriment—Too focused on the mundane. No pleasure or enjoyment in your life. Dogmatic and critical person. Fear and inability to manifest on the physical plane. Attend to physical health.

King of Pentacles

The King sits on his throne surrounded by many symbols. The two signs of Taurus the bull adorn his throne on both sides. In one hand he holds his tool and in the other a pentacle. Abundance surrounds him. He is confident and powerful in making ideas reality.

Positive Meaning—A man of great power and material wealth. Practicality in the ability to channel ideas into reality. Industry, business or financial success. A person to help you gain a material desire. Marriage. Responsibility. Father figure. Advisor. Consultant. Manager.

Detriment—Seek the help of an experienced advisor. Avoid greed and narrow minded action. Build a base before starting action. Balance spiritual, and mental desires with material desires. Be more economical.

The Tarot Reading

The best part of experiencing the tarot is the actual reading. A reading is of course the process through which you gather information from the cards. The reading is the core of the tarot activity.

There are actually several different methods for reading your cards. We will discuss some of the terms and give you enough insight to begin. The best thing about the tarot is that it soon will begin to wear your special brand. That is, both the meanings of the cards and the spreads themselves start to individualize as you interact with them. You will end up adding your own special touches to your readings as time progresses.

If you read for someone else, you are the reader and that person is the *querist*. The information received from the cards should be information concerning the querist. Your influence in the matter should be as neutral as possible. This is an important point. Since they rely on you to interpret the cards, it is important that your personal biases and perspectives stay out of the reading.

There is a part of you that should be in the reading. The more you know about the cards and their symbols, the better you will be able to interpret them. As the reader, it is your primary responsibility to allow the question to come from the querist and clearly reflect the answer from the cards.

Before you do your reading, try to free yourself of tensions and any anxiety you may have. By taking a few deep breaths, and relaxing for a moment, you will be able to clear your subconscious channels. Never read when you are angry, upset, or anxious. You will be more prone to manipulate the information rather than accepting it as it really is. The more you read, the more the cards will speak to you.

Do not force information from the cards. If you ask a question, be patient and wait for the answer. There are some times when the cards will refuse to answer a question. This is an answer in itself. It is telling you that this is not the time to ask this particular question. Or it may mean that you should re-phrase the question. In doing so you will focus more directly on what you really mean.

As you develop the proper questions you begin to deal the cards. As you search for the meanings, you begin to uncover the truth in a given situation.

Meanings to your readings will be easier using this book. Each card has been selectively explained to offer you the most practical and to the point definition. It is up to you to associate and connect those meanings to your particular situations.

As I said before, do not force an answer from the cards. You can continue to ask and rephrase questions, but know when it is time to stop a reading and approach it at another time.

The treatment of your cards is important. Keep them in a safe place. It is advisable to wrap them in a piece of cloth, perhaps silk or cotton. The more caring, and sincerely you interact with your cards, the better they will treat you. If you have a favorite process of meditation or spiritual ceremony that you would like to apply to the storage of your cards, feel free to do so. They will eventually closely reflect your touch, sight, and intuitive senses.

When you do your readings, you will create what is called a spread. A spread is the actual pattern you create when you lay out your cards. It literally refers to the way you spread your cards in front of you. There are five different spreads suggested in this book. Each is designed to give you clear and concise information. As you develop, you will no doubt create a favorite spread. The spreads offered here are the most effective and will give you hours of tarot pleasure.

Make sure you are reading in a place conducive for the information to flow through. I have even done readings while on an airplane or in a restaurant. It is more important for you to be able to relate to the cards.

Some people have a special place in the home designated as a sort of spiritual area. The use of incense, lighting, colors, and music may or may not help. It all depends on you. Of course any area filled with noise, cigarette smoke, and confusion is not the best area. Your cards are sensitive. They pick up vibrations from you and your environment. Treat them with care.

Phrasing your question to the cards is important. As the thought becomes clearer, so is the tarot response. Be as specific as you can with your questions. If you have them in mind use names, dates, places or things. At the same time avoid making your questions long and wordy. The tarot appreciates it if you get to the point. At first you may find your questions are a bit off the mark. They may be somewhat vague and general. Do not be afraid of asking it in a different way if you feel the tarot did not respond to it in your first reading. As you dig deeper into the subconscious response, your questions will automatically develop.

Also keep in mind, there are several meanings for each card. Apply the meaning and category that best suits your question. Mind you, I did not say interpret the cards to your advantage. This is manipulation of the cards. Just because they did not give you the answer you wanted, do not manipulate the information. There is another way to shape your desired outcome.

Through meditation and visualization, you can begin to reshape a less than desirable outcome. Let's create an example.

A question concerning a loved one may be phrased like this: Dear Tarot, My loved one and I are experiencing difficulties. What is the root of these problems? The tarot hypothetically shows there is selfish self—centered behavior on the part of one person (Devil in detriment). Further probing shows you that this is due to a lack of faith in the relationship. You then may restart and ask another question. Who is the person? The tarot shows it is you. You then may restart and ask what you can do about it? When the tarot answers with the Strength, it shows you must have inner fortitude and physical energy. This may mean you are not doing the small things that make a relationship work on the material plane. Perhaps the feelings are there and you feel there is a mental and spiritual connection. Physical energy in the relationship means you must demonstrate your love through action. Saying and feeling the love is not enough. You must learn to show it more.

It is possible to then take the Strength card and create a visualization. Put it in front of you. Read the total meaning of the card. Visualize the essence of the lion. The energy and fortitude of the Strength. See yourself as gaining these traits. Also repeat the expression that is pertinent of Strength. It will help you internalize the essence of its meaning. Through visualization and applying the information given in the special features, you will be able to internalize the personality of a given card.

You will notice in the definitions the words positive meaning and detriment are used. The positive meaning relates if the card is selected right side up. The detriment relates to the card if it is upside down. Depending on your reading, you may only want to place your cards in the deck right side up. In the definitions I have purposely presented the positive side of both positions. Many tarot books present a hopeless, no win frame of mind by telling you many negative things concerning the meanings. Just because a card is upside down, it does not mean the situation is hopeless. In fact it may be just the opposite. This should let you know what you must do to turn a situation around. How you can improve yourself and the situation in question. Both the positive meaning and the detriment position are designed to give information concerning times, dates, numbers, and the people involved in the issue. While some answers will let you know that all is well, keep going straight ahead, others will let you know you should move in another direction.

The spreads move from the least detailed to the more detailed. The quick look spread can include two, three or four cards. The more detailed spreads include up to seven eleven and thirteen cards.

The Celtic Cross

This spread is one of the most widely used and is a favorite of many professional readers. It is the place you will begin to learn the meaning of the cards in application. One good reason for its popularity is its depth and thoroughness.

When you begin any reading shuffle your cards. Then place them in front of you face down, until it is time to lay out your spread. As you lay the cards down, turn them face up to view them. If reading for yourself, you then cut the deck into three sections. If reading for another,

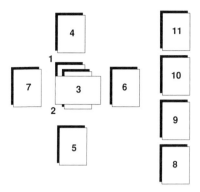

have them shuffle and cut them. Place the cards back together in a different order than they originally were.

Lay them out following the diagram of the cross. As you place each card down say to yourself the meaning of each position.

Card one — This card is selected by you before the others are pulled from the deck. In the center place this card. It represents the querist. Select the card that best represents the personality of the person seeking the reading. If a man usually a king or one of the male Major Arcana. If a woman usually a queen or one of the female Major Arcana. Read the personalities and the meanings of the cards to find out which card best represents the querist. This will apply to all the readings to come.

2. Cover — This is the card that represents the subject in question. This is the essence of your question. It also reflects the temperament and the conditions that influence the question.

3. Crosses — Lay this card across the second card. It is a short term solution to the question. It also represents the obstacles or energies that are working in opposition to the question. The positive meaning of this card is always selected. Use this card to find out what is or what may potentially stop the progress.

4. Above—This card shows the possible results. It is a general idea of the results that can be obtained. Things are not solid yet, but this is a general idea of the potential as things are unfolding in the reading.

5. Below—Your past. This is the foundation of the question. Things that have already happened to affect the matter. Usually people, places or things in the past that have made the situation what it is. Often you can call on this element to support you. Or you may want to break away from it.

6. The past—These events are leaving from your life. They are near completion as a new phase is about to begin. Whatever the influences are, they are now changing. This is the immediate past.

7. In front—These issues are coming to fruition now or in the immediate future. They are the influences that will surround you as the past fades into the background.

8. You or your question—This card, started in a separate row, is descriptive of you or your question. It is a detailed look at your true feelings, and the nature of the question.

9. Peers—This is a look at the feelings and actions of other people around you. Especially family members, friends, or co-workers. It also relates to the environment around you.

10. Hopes, fears—This card relates to the card that crosses. It is your innermost desires. Hopes and fears come alive in this card.

11. Outcome—This is the final outcome of the issue. The results as the situation exists. If this card is unclear you may proceed to turn over one more card for additional information. Remember this is only the outcome as the situation currently exists. You do have the power through the information you have received to move your destiny into a more positive direction. Do however be careful that you do not tamper with the natural order of things. Some things are best left as they are.

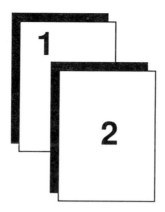

The Instant Spread

This spread is not so much designed to save you time as it is designed to give you an instantaneous, basic answer to your question.

Card one—As always select the card that best represents either your question or the querist. If your question concerns romantic relationships, use the Lovers. If it is regarding employment, use the Chariot. If it concerns financial dealings try the Wheel of Fortune. These are only suggestions. Try the card that best represents your interpretation of the issue at hand.

Card two—After shuffling and cutting the cards, cover the first card. This card will answer your question.

Past, Present, Future

This is a three card spread that will allow you to look at the past developments, the current status, and the future outlook of an issue. As you do this reading, keep in mind that the information you receive should help you elevate your situation or advance it in some manner. Do not allow your readings to influence your life to the point that you become dependent on their answers. Your destiny can be altered to a positive direction if you so choose. Or you can brood, blame others, and hold on to negative patterns if you so choose. The decision is up to you.

In this reading there is a direct chance for you to observe the progression of your life. The past will tell the issues that you have already faced. The present will tell you what is going on with an issue at the present moment. The future will tell you where an issue may be headed, based on the current circumstances.

The Intuitive Spread

This spread is a free form spread that does not require a specific issue or focus. The purpose is to allow the cards to tell you whatever there is for them to share with you. The question may be phrased as such: Dear Tarot Cards, is there anything you would like to share with me concerning my life?

Card one—Romance. This is relationships, husband, wife, sweetheart, or a developing relationship.

Card two—Finances. This card will speak to monetary issues, and material possessions.

Card three—Health and well-being. This card relates to physical, emotional, and spiritual health issues.

Card four—Career/job. This card relates to career opportunities, and employment.

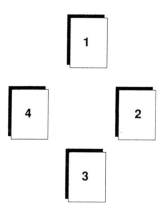

The Development Spread

The Development spread was discovered in the practice of a tarot teacher and healer who apprised me of its effectiveness. It is a spread that focuses on the creative and intuitive energies. It is especially great for removing creative blocks and for the initiation of creative projects. Also for those who seek the intervention of spiritual influences in their work, this spread will be a good one to work with.

card one—today

card two—yesterday

card three—tomorrow

card four—creative influences on yesterday

card five—intuitive influences on yesterday

card six—creative influences on tomorrow

card seven—intuitive influences on tomorrow

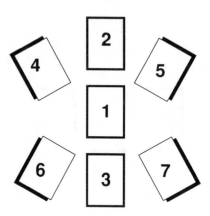

The Horoscope Spread

This is also a most effective spread. The horoscope is divided into twelve signs and twelve houses. Each of the signs has a certain influence on our lives. They affect our personalities, health, desires and relationships. Below is a short description of each area and its influence. When completing this spread apply the meanings of each card position to the description given below.

Card S—This is the significance or the querist. It is the main energy in the reading

Card one—Aries. The first house. The first action. How the world sees you. Your personality in its growth and development. What your undeveloped skills may be. Self image, head and face.

Card two—Taurus. Your financial and material possessions. How you may earn income. What your attitude is about financial development. Self esteem, throat and neck.

Card three—Gemini—Early education. Communication issues. What you think in your mind and how you think. Brothers and sisters, and short trips are relative in this house. Processing facts. Education. Arms, lungs, hands.

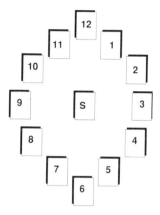

Card four — Cancer. Parents. Family situations. All domestic affairs. Property. Chest and stomach.

Card five — Leo. Your creative activities. Drama, entertainment and pleasures. Also, children are represented here. Romance. Heart and spine.

Card six — Virgo. This rules the area of pets, health and the service you offer to others. Every day activities. Responsibilities. Colon.

Card seven — Libra. The area of friendships, partnerships and physical beauty. Contracts. Kidneys.

Card eight — Scorpio. A card that will represent, sexual activities, resources and ambitions. Many lessons are to be learned in this area. Rebirth and death. Insurance and personal insight. Sexual organs.

Card nine — Sagittarius — Higher education and honesty. It also relates to spiritual development and philosophy and religion, law, philosophy, hips and thighs.

Card ten — Capricorn. A card of future development and stability, it represents your career advancements, and your ability to overcome obstacles. Business. Knees.

Card eleven—Aquarius. House of friends and associates. It is your desire to connect with humanitarian issues, inventions and scientific pursuits. It tells of your personal goals. Hopes and desires. Legs and ankles.

Additional Suggestions

1. When interpreting your cards, never be disillusioned with the results. Do not feel hopeless or negative. The cards will tell you the environment surrounding an issue. This may be used as an encouragement to break through the obstacles, as well as an indicator of the obstacles themselves.

2. Whether you are reading for yourself or reading for another, try to remain objective. Allow the cards the space and time to project their true meaning.

3. Take your time when you do your spread. Study each card, until you have grasped the meaning. Then go on to the next card. Often, you may let the spread rest for a moment or for a day and come back to it several times. Each time your understanding of its information will expand.

4. Write your readings down. Take notes on them and compare. You may notice patterns or connections between the readings.

5. For more convincing results, try reading the cards with all the Major Arcana only. Another suggestion is to use the cards in only the Positive meaning position (right side up).

6. Instead of shuffling and cutting the cards three times, try the random selection technique. Place all the cards on the table in front of you. Swish them around and mix them up thoroughly. One by one, pick the cards from the pile in front of you. Create your spreads intuitively.

Numbers and the Tarot

The relationship of numbers to the understanding of the tarot is an important one. Each of the cards has a numerical value. The numbers one to nine make an interesting observation in applying them to our readings. When a number is over ten, reduce it by adding the two numbers together. For example 12 is equal to 1 + 2 = 3. Below are some of the meanings to help you interpret your readings.

One—This is the universal, primal number. It is the beginning of all things. Initiation, primal energy force, power, self reliance, individuality, inner confidence, leadership, manifestation, independence, unity, manifestation, action, tarot cards are—Magician, all Aces, Sun, all tens.

Two—This is the number of partnership and co-operation. It also represents balance, harmony, co-operation, diplomacy, peace, organization, art, perfection, duality, togetherness, reality, sexual energy. Tarot cards are High Priestess, Justice, all two's, all Pages, and the Judgment.

Three—This is the number of completions. It is also combinations, synthesis, energy, administration, fulfillment, entertainment, mental energy, evolution, emotions, pyramidal energy. The tarot cards are Empress, Hanged Man, World, all threes, all knights.

Four—This is the number of the square. It is the number of perfection, physical and material world, conservative, systems, logic, structure, discipline. The tarot cards are Emperor, Death, all fours and all queens.

Five—This is a number of freedom, wholeness, humanity, expression, senses, temptation. Tarot cards are Hierophant, Temperance, all fives, and all kings.

Six—This number is the symbol of progress and development. It also represents synergy and a turn for the better. Equilibrium, service, and wisdom. Tarot cards are the Lovers, Devil, and all sixes.

Seven—This is the number of inner development. It also represents spirituality, reflection, education, stability, influence, integrity, and perfection. The tarot cards are Chariot, Tower, and all sevens.

Eights—This number represents continuity, resolutions, material wealth, power, possessiveness, business, and organization. The tarot cards are Strength, Star, and all eights.

Nine—The nines represent endings and satisfaction. They are also the universe, completion, humanity, idealism, rest, and truth. The tarot cards are Hermit, Moon, and all nines.

There are remarkable connections in the system of numbers as they relate to the tarot. Pay attention to the cards in each number and make these connections for yourself. They will unlock many secrets for you. Through this application you will be able to see the relationship of all cards to one another.

Colors and the Tarot

You will notice that your tarot cards are colorful. Each color has a meaning. As you read your cards, the colors will speak to you along with the images, numbers, and their given definitions. Below are a few of the meanings. They should be considered when you complete your spreads.

Red—Strength and vitality, stimulating, sexual stimulant, courage, increases vibrations, dynamic energy, hot, passion, affection and love, destruction, warning, excitement, anger, fire, rage.

Orange—Warming, energy, stimulating, respiration, spiritual attunement, activity, intellectual and reproductive energy integrated, harmonizing, enlivening, pride, ambition, energy, loneliness, fear, hope, suspicion, insecurity, bad habits, hope.

Yellow—Intellect and brain power, radiance, respiratory, muscles, stimulant, enthusiasm, nervous system, diversity, originality, self-expression, oral communication, perception, jealousy, shame, dishonor, creativity, adapting to change, luminosity, sunshine, analysis, optimism.

Green—Harmony, and balance, health and well-being, fertility, new life, growth, charity, youth, relaxation, peace, hope, adaptation, reflection, luck, good fortune, consistency, wisdom, high vibrations, heart, love, nature, abundance, detail, healing.

Blue—Inner peace and friendship, serenity, inspiration, relaxing, calming, soothing, water, emotions, honesty, nobility, spirituality, meditation, philosophy, security, truth, clarity, communication, speech, intuition, faith, devotion, sincerity, travel.

Violet/purple—Vision, insight, royalty, inspiration, intuition, psychic, exploration, depression, relaxing, devotion, worship, ascension, unity, god-like, transformation, higher self, sadness, sentimental, religion, justice, fairness, expansion, family.

Black—Change, release, renewal

White—protection, unity, attachment

Rainbow—harmony, miracles, balance

Astrological Rulers of Major Arcana

0. Fool	Air
1. Magician	Mercury
2. High Priestess	Moon
3. Empress	Venus
4. Emperor	Aries
5. Hierophant	Taurus
6. Lovers	Gemini
7. Chariot	Cancer
8. Strength	Leo
9. Hermit	Virgo
10. Wheel of Fortune	Jupiter
11. Justice	Libra
12. Hanged Man	Water
13. Death	Scorpio
14. Temperance	Sagittarius
15. Devil	Capricorn
16. Tower	Mars
17. Star	Aquarius
18. Moon	Pisces
19. Sun	Sun
20. Judgment	Fire
21. World	Saturn/Pluto

Summary

Into the future we go! The future of self analysis and personal development promises to be an active one.

The word holistic is a term that refers to the entire body. The tarot can be of help in both locating and preventing imbalances in our lives. The goal of achieving happiness and well being is balance. A balance of all our forces.

Each individual has the potential to achieve greatness in some phase of their life. This may be as a parent, as a teacher, as a student, or in the career area. Our skills, knowledge, and activities are often over-shadowed because of fears and insecurities. The tarot can teach us to move beyond fears and express the real self. The true self can surface from the subconscious, into the conscious. It comes to the surface and we become aware of who we really are.

The future can be a bright one. The tools for all we need exist within our reach. As we walk, grow, and live together, it is my hope that humanity will respond to the need for global peace and technological development.

Together, the yin and the yang, the male and the female, the logical and the intuitive will blend together to create a synergy of the highest human order — an order that links our purpose with the reflection of the God-like principle in each of us.

The discovery of this principle begins with the discovery of the true self. An inner journey, I am sure you will enjoy.

Celtic Spread

Intuitive Spread

Development Spread

Instant Spread

Horoscope Spread

Past, Present, Future Spread